GW01018577

Conte

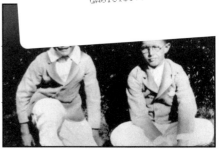

RE 16|6 99p

President Bush has always prefered pitching to catching.

★

"*George Bush was born on third base and thinks he hit a triple.* "

John Hightower

George Herbert Walker Bush as Jo in the Bush family production of "Little Women" (age 8)

★

Chapter 1

Born to Run Things

THIS IS A REPUBLIC, NOT A DEMOCRACY!" thundered Prescott Sheldon "The Prez" Bush. It was a sunny Sunday morning in the spring of 1934. The entire Bush family and its retinue were assembled in the spacious drawing-room of the Bush mansion on Grove Lane in fashionable, exclusive Greenwich, Connecticut. To "The Prez"'s right was his healthy, energetic and neatly turned-out family. First and foremost his lovely, faithful and athletic wife, Dorothy "Mumsy" Bush. Then, of course, his adoring, orderly, obedient, and well-mannered children: his eldest son, Prescott "Presky" Bush Jr., "Presky"'s kid brother, George "Poppy" Bush, "Presky" and "Poppy"'s kid sister, Nancy "Nancy" Bush, and little Jonathan "Shut The Baby Up" Bush. Last but not least, their beloved mutt, Stalin. To his left were numerous Bush family servants, many of whom were known simply by jolly nicknames like "Bonkers" and "You." The most important servants were the Bushes' two Negro maids, "George" and "Herbert" and their Negro butler, "Walker the Butler."

The tall, powerfully built, clean-jawed, blue-eyed, handsome, strict, fair, honest, thrifty, well-bred, presti-gious, influential, and deservedly prosperous Prescott Sheldon "The Prez" Bush had a custom. Every Sunday morning after attending services at the beautiful Episcopal church located within easy walking distance of their home, he would read aloud from some improving book. This morning it had been "Turn the Other Fender: A Guide to Christian Driving," by his old Yalie chum, Rev. Mackintosh "Flasher" Whitney-Combemartin III.

Sunday morning was a time, too, when the achievements of the week were rewarded and the failures punished. Everyone would quake. While they all trusted his judgment without question, they could never be sure that they'd lived up to his

Poppy was cared for as a child by two devoted Negro maids: George (left) and Herbert (right).

tremendously high standards."A republic is like an orderly, clean-living, well-trained body," continued the paterfamilias, "while a democracy is like a bunch of drunk–bog-paddies in a bar."

Family and servants alike enjoyed a hearty laugh at this sally. One of "The Prez"'s saving graces— not that he needed any—was his nifty sense of humor.

"This family is no different. This family is an orderly, clean-living, well-trained body—not a bunch of drunk–bog-paddies in a bar!"

The elder Bush paused for effect. His mellifluous speaking voice, together with his enviable talent for organizing his thoughts, had garnered many awards from such worthy organizations as the Elks, the Freemasons and the Aryan Knights of Perpetual Liberty.

"I am the head of this body." declared the patriarch. "Dorothy 'Mumsy' Bush is the heart. 'Presky,' 'Poppy,' 'Nancy,' et cetera, my devoted children, are the vital organs. For example, George here is the kidneys. And you faithful retainers are the arms, legs, fingers and feet of this body."

"Papa, am I 'Setra'?" lisped Baby Jonathan.

"QUIET!" roared the Prez, tapping the toddler back into line with a polo mallet.

"Now sometimes" he continued, "the arms and legs and fingers act in a so-called democratic manner. They act on impulse, for their own selfish, short-term ends. They omit due consultation with the head, who alone can comprehend and determine all the long-term interests of the body!"

★

Fear passed like a riptide through the assembled servants.

"Let's say that you, Walker the Butler, are the fingers of this little republic," said the Prez, turning to the faithful Negro who had been with the family for many generations.

"Ise proud to be yo' fingers, Mass' Bush," said the stout fellow in his quaint lingo.

"Let's say those fingers stray some night into one of the republic's most precious assets, the Napoleon brandy in the crystal decanter in the dining-room!"

"Ise ain't never touch a drop, Mass' Bush. Never. Jesus tole me not to," muttered the unrepentant darkie.

"Then I the head," went on his wrathful master, hitting the errant Negro about the head and shoulders with a royal court tennis racquet, "say to the fingers, go! Go up to the back bathroom on the second floor and...UNPLUG THAT BLOCKED TOILET WITH YOUR BARE HANDS!"

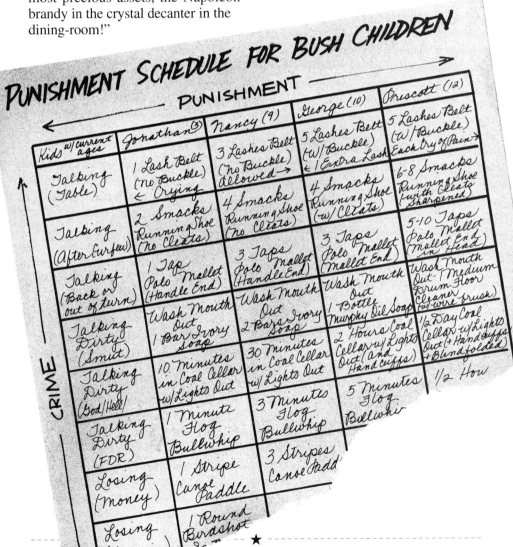

PUNISHMENT SCHEDULE FOR BUSH CHILDREN

CRIME \ Kids w/current ages	Jonathan (3)	Nancy (9)	George (10)	Prescott (12)
Talking (Table)	1 Lash Belt (no Buckle) ← Crying	3 Lashes Belt (no Buckle) allowed →	5 Lashes Belt (w/ Buckle)	5 Lashes Belt (w/ Buckle) Each Cry of Pain → + 1 Extra Lash
Talking (After Curfew)	2 Smacks Running Shoe (no Cleats)	4 Smacks Running Shoe (no Cleats)	4 Smacks Running Shoe (w/ Cleats)	6-8 Smacks Running Shoe (with Cleats Sharpened)
Talking (Back or out of turn)	1 Tap Polo Mallet (Handle End)	3 Taps Polo Mallet (Handle End)	3 Taps Polo Mallet (Mallet End)	5-10 Taps Polo Mallet (Mallet End in Head)
Talking Dirty (Smut)	Wash Mouth Out 1 Bar Ivory Soap	Wash Mouth Out 2 Bars Ivory Soap	Wash Mouth Out 1 Bottle Murphy Oil Soap	Wash Mouth Out 1 Medium Drum Floor Cleaner (w/ wire brush)
Talking Dirty (God/Hell)	10 Minutes in Coal Cellar w/ Lights Out	30 Minutes in Coal Cellar w/ Lights Out	2 Hours Coal Cellar w/ Lights Out (and Handcuffs)	1/2 Day Coal Cellar w/ Lights Out (+ Handcuffs + Blindfolded)
Talking Dirty (FDR)	1 Minute Flog Bullwhip	3 Minutes Flog Bullwhip	5 Minutes Flog Bullwhip	1/2 Hour
Losing (Money)	1 Stripe Canoe Paddle	3 Stripes Canoe Paddle		
Losing (Tennis)	1 Round Birdshot			

Young Poppy Bush adored his father. From such lessons as these he learned all he would one day need to know to run his own republic. And though the "head" often reinforced the lessons learned by the "kidneys" with the buckle of a Brooks Brothers belt, Poppy bore no grudge. Because these beatings were given with love, he learned to endure, and eventually enjoy, them.

Without question his pedigree gave him the moral fiber to absorb enormous physical pain. His father was a third-generation American of English descent who could trace his ancestry back to Henry III, King of England. This made his children thirteenth cousins once removed of the future Elizabeth II. It's thrilling to ponder that if only 343 members of the British Royal Family and their relatives were to die —if, say, they were all on the same 747 and it blew up mysteriously in mid-air—Poppy Bush would not only be President of the United States but Queen of England as well.

But no one should imagine that the Bushes lived on Easy Street. The Bush children would often look at pictures of the terrible economic Depression in the exciting new magazine *Life*.

His father of course had no truck with the Democrats and their ringleader, the possibly Jewish Roosevelt.

"Poppy!" the Prez would some-times call out at the breakfast table. "In this house does NRA mean the National Recovery Administration?"

"No, sir!" young Poppy would answer "In this household it means the National Rifle Association!"

Then his father would beam with pleasure. And instead of the belt, Poppy would get another share of General Electric Preferred.

The future President was no pampered child of luxury. He was five before he got his own set of golf clubs. He and Presky had to share the same sailboat for years.

> **The future President was no pampered child of luxury. He was five before he got his own set of golf clubs. He and Presky had to share the same sailboat for years.**

One thing that obsessed Poppy as a boy was that he was physically very small. Knowing his father would often beat people just for being puny, he strove mightily to increase his height, spending many painful hours hanging in the garage from a harness with thirty-pound dumbbells attached to his feet.

Like most boys of their background, Poppy and Presky had a two-story, six-bedroom treehouse in one of the majestic oaks that graced the Bush estate. In theory it was for the whole family, but the two older boys quickly made it their own and— except when they wanted to play doctor—kept their sister out. To this day, the President's nifty treehouse memories make him question whether the so-called "opening-up" of private clubs isn't in the long run self-defeating.

★

Despite their wealth, the Bushes never spoiled their children.
Poppy had to share this treehouse with his brother Presky.
(The servants' quarters were in a different tree.)

★

Greenwich police knew Poppy and Presky Bush as "The Smarty Boys." The amateur detectives solved scores of mysteries, putting many a Bolshevik hobo behind bars.

Poppy and Presky would often raid their mother's Kelvinator for a secret treehouse feast. Their only criterion was that everything they ate had to be white. They liked mashed potatoes, macaroni and cheese, vanilla ice-cream, marshmallows, popcorn, milk, bread, lima beans, chicken breasts, cauliflower, mayonnaise (with everything), coconut, whipped cream, cream cheese, cottage- cheese, noodles, rice pudding, and meringues.

But not whitefish.

Herbert, the Negro maid they shared, would oftentimes be blamed when food went missing from the Kelvinator. Poppy and Presky would share a hearty laugh when their father punished Herbert, for she was generously endowed in her rear portions. But they would always own up afterwards and take their medicine like men.

From observing Herbert, the young future leaders learned an

★

interesting lesson in Politics. They realized that not all Americans wanted the "freedom" so-called democracy promised them. Herbert, they noticed, never voted, and if she had, there would been no one of her ilk for her to vote for. The Prez explained this conundrum one day. Elections were a cruel hoax, he told his sons. Most common people, he averred, people like Herbert, wanted only to be told what to do and how much they were getting paid for it. They would no more miss elections, if there were none, than they would miss caviar.

Some people were Born to Run Things, most were not. That was that.

In the summer and at Christmas, the entire Bush family and their favorite servants left the "city"— Greenwich—to go to the "country." In summer it was Kennebunkport, Maine; in winter, Duncannon in South Carolina. Unlike real rich people, the Bushes didn't own these lavish second and third homes. They were merely allowed to use them by "Mumsy"'s father "Pops" Walker.

It was on one of these Christmas visits that Poppy and Presky had the first of many exciting adventures.

It was Christmas Eve and a turkey was missing from their grandfather's large, well-run turkey farm. Poppy and Presky were deter-

mined to solve the mystery and hunt the culprit down.

Just like real detectives, they searched the turkey farm for clues. Soon they found what they were looking for—footprints in the snow, leading from the turkey barn. Better still, the tracks were of a man with one shoe and one bare foot. Now they could identify the suspect!

Excitedly the two boys followed the tracks, and just as night fell, they came upon a pair of hoboes near the railroad yards. Sure enough, they were roasting a turkey on a spit over a campfire. But how could the two sleuths be sure this was the stolen turkey? And which of the two hoboes was the thief?

Cautiously the plucky duo crept closer. By the flickering light of the campfire they noticed that each of the hoboes had only one leg! One hobo's good leg sported a battered shoe. The other hobo's good leg had no shoe at all! They boys had solved the mystery!

Quick as a flash the young detectives slipped away, called the police and had the hoboes arrested. The hobo with no shoe was sentenced to five years' hard labor, while his pal turned state's evidence and only got three. Meanwhile the turkey was restored to its rightful owner and the boys were rewarded with a hundred shares each of General Electric Preferred. ∎

> *Most common people, he averred, people like Herbert the maid, wanted only to be told what to do and how much they were getting paid for it.*

A fragile, winsome, doe-like beauty, Poppy went through Andover in mortal fear his classmates would find him irresistibly attractive.

★

Up Andover

I N 1936, TWELVE-YEAR-OLD POPPY embarked on the second stage of the rugged dirt road that would one day bring him to the White House. He was enrolled at Phillips Academy, a stately, ivy-clad school often called Andover after the sleepy somewhat vulgar little town it graces with its presence. Happily, brother "Presky" was already enrolled. The siblings were reunited and quickly assumed the mantle of Most Popular Newcomers, being known to their classmates as the Bush Leaguers.

There was so much to do! There were boodle-boxes to be opened and their contents bargained for. There were beds to be short-sheeted and boys with glasses to be made fun of. There were arguments to be settled over who had the stupid-est chauffeur.

Harmless schoolboy witticisms abounded. Poppy learnt that Harriet Beecher Stowe—the great American writer who is buried at Andover— was always referred to as Harriet Beecher Meat. Andover's home state meanwhile had to be pronounced "Massa-two-shits." Woe betide the boy who used the correct forms! He'd have a painful Indian rub in store!

But there was a sad side to the jolly boyish mayhem. This was the first time young Poppy had ever lived away from home. For a while he reverted to a disgusting habit he'd had as a small child—fainting in public and then vomiting on the nearest person's lap.

There was an unfortunate result of the loathsome vomiting incidents. In a rare rift between the brothers over some long-forgotten trifle, Presky let it be known to the class that the regurgitative fits were the source of George's nickname, Poppy. Mumsy Bush used to refer to her second son's habit of collapsing and puking as "popping." In fact his original nickname had been "Projectile Poppy."

To compensate for this effeminacy, Poppy set out to project a manly image. He went out for every sport offered by the stately old school, and soon excelled in baseball, basketball, swimming, soccer, diving, long

★

Puny as a young boy, Poppy increased his height dramatically by hanging from a harness in the school crypt with thirty-pound dumbbells attached to his feet.

★

jump, high jump, 100-yard dash, discus, javelin, shot put, sailing, rowing, tennis, court tennis, squash, handball, fives, hunting shooting, lacrosse, field hockey, ice hockey, curling, quoits, rugger, polo, fencing, billiards, dominos, and darts. But it was not enough. He redoubled his efforts to stretch his body to normal height. It worked. Soon he was the tallest boy in his class. Alas, this only intensified the fragile willowy beauty of his stunningly handsome good looks.

Poppy endured his teenage years at Andover in mortal fear that he would be found attractive by other boys. Or worse still, by the masters, many of whom were from unsavory backgrounds. Some were even Noël Coward fans.

He need not have worried. The other boys may have found him attractive. (Such things are hardly surprising in a group whose fathers could afford the most beautiful women in the land). But they were in awe of him. Poppy displayed early on the attributes of a born leader. For example, he knew how to expand his capital by managing the capital of his classmates.

Here's how it worked: His father gave him an allowance of a hundred and ten dollars a month. Poppy would lend this money to all comers—fellows from good backgrounds who lacked self-control, smoked cigarettes behind the chapel, or snuck out to go drinking with the hayseeds in town.

Poppy soon discovered that there were more boys requiring loans than he could accommodate. Realizing that many boys, especially wonks and geeks, had allowances they were not spending, he set out to persuade them to let him manage their money.

Poppy reinvested a portion of his earnings by hiring wonks to do his schoolwork. (thus ensuring himself high grades and an increased allowance). In some cases, of course, these were the same wonks whose capital he was managing. He was ensuring growth, while investing in R&D, as well as creating both capital gains and employment!

Thus did the clean-jawed, clear-eyed boys of Andover learn the realities of economic life. The strong links of future leadership were forged in the furnace of an embryonic, unregulated Savings and Loan System.

Friendships too were formed in the pell-mell of "puppy" finance and harmless prep-school high jinks. Once, for example, during grouse-shooting practice, Poppy accidentally blew another boy's buttock off.

The lad in question bore Poppy no ill-will. He knew the shooting had been an accident. As it happened, he owed the future President $27.33. The debt was promptly repaid.

> ### Friendships too were formed in the pell-mell of 'Puppy' finance and harmless prep-school hi-jinks. Once for example, during grouse-shooting practice, Poppy accidentally blew another boy's buttock off.

★

When Poppy became Vice-President, the two renewed their friendship, and the man now sits—albeit somewhat awkwardly—on many of the nation's most powerful boards and secret committees.

During Christmas vacation 1941, Poppy—by now a tall, lissome seventeen-year-old —attended a cotillion at the Round Hill Country Club in Greenwich. For the young squires of Greenwich, it was the first sight they had of the young maidens of town. How the girls had blossomed at their own exclusive boarding schools! The ballroom was aglow with their pale beauty and the mature elegance of their chaperones.

The handsome young "Bush

The "city boy" from Greenwich was right at home "down on the farm" in Massachusetts. Here Poppy is shown with his pet chicken "Oinker." (P.S.: The eggs tasted terrible!)

★

Poppy's graduation picture. Top row left to right: John Leopold, Whittaker Leopold, Clayton "Muffcakes" Leopold, Sydney Leopold III, Dryden Leopold-Leopold, Lord Leopold of Strangling. Bottom row left to right: Fred Loeb, George Herbert Walker Bush, Thurston Loeb, Fitzhugh "Fizzywizzy" Loeb, Pattinson Wilkinson Parkinson Loeb Jr., Baron Wilhelm von Fruntl-Loeb.

boy" who—other than "Mumsy" sister Nancy, and Herbert—had little experience of women, was enthralled. He felt like a bull in a candy store.

"There they were," he recalls, "all these beautiful creatures in long dresses with big bumps in front."

One of the beautiful creatures in particular caught Poppy's attention. She was an attractive brunette in an off-the-shoulder dress with an impressive athletic build. But what drew Poppy to Barbara Pierce most was her exceptionally large, curvaceous bumps.

Poppy has never forgotten their first dance.

"I'm sure the dance floor was crowded," he recalls, "but as the music played it felt like we were the only people in the world! Just me and Barbara and her chaperone."

As the trio glided gracefully beneath the merry but tasteful decorations, Poppy knew he was falling in love. When the music ended they found themselves, alone now, under a sprig of mistletoe. Poppy drew a deep breath and asked for a kiss.

His first kiss! Here he was a mere seventeen years old, at his first cotillion, and he had met the girl of his dreams! The tension was unbearable. For a moment he thought he might "pop," but happily the moment passed.

The chaperone gave her consent to the kiss. Their lips met.

"I forget her name" says Poppy now. "She had three, like all Greenwich women. And a slight moustache."

The chaperone passed the kiss on to the breathless debutante. And as she shyly accepted, two hearts were joined forever.   ∎

★

Lieutenant Bush is rescued from almost certain dehydration by the submarine *Finback* after spending more than 7000 seconds afloat in a standard-issue Navy liferaft, which could have sprung a leak if attacked by a shark or a giant squid, or capsized if a violent typhoon had blown up. (If Bush had not been rescued by the submarine, it would have been almost an hour before another vessel passed his way—plenty of time for a shark or typhoon to do its dirty work.)

★

How I Won The War

THEY CAME IN AT TEN thousand feet and slipped into a shallow dive. Avengers, the Grumman Corporation called the bulky bombers, but to the tough, terse, good-humored men of the aircraft carrier *San Jacinto*, they were "Pregnant Turkeys," The huge single-engined planes were hurtling relentlessly towards their target: an immensely vital radio transmitter atop Mount Yoake on a tiny island in the Bonins called Chichi Jima. It was September 2, 1944.

A forest of Jap ack-ack guns snarled their defiance. The air was thick with flak. Undaunted, the Yank bombers stayed on beam, four avenging angels plunging from the sky.

Eight thousand ... seven thousand ... six ... five ... four ...

Lieutenant Poppy was Number Three in the bombing sequence. Any second now Squadron Leader Don "Yes Sir!" Melvin would release his four five-hundred-pound parcels of fiery death.

There they went! Direct hit! Sayonara, Jap transmitter! Poppy's heart burst with pride as he watched West, Number Two, zero in on the same target. KERWHOP! went the bombs. Another hit! The world exploded into smoke and flame. Could he be that close to the target?

Check the altimeter. Golly, where's the altimeter? Hey, that smoke isn't the transmitter! That's my wings!

We've been hit!

Drop the bombs! No good! Still losing altitude! Yikes! Get out, get out get out!

Wait. That wasn't what you said on a plane. It was something else, but it had slipped his mind...

Scram? Scoot? Skedaddle? Goshdarn, what was Navy lingo for getting of out a plane in a hurry?

His Avenger looked like a Flaming Turkey now. Surely White and Delaney—his gunner and radioman—surely they could see the flames. They'd know the term. Perhaps he could ask them. No, wait! He was supposed to tell them. He was the pilot.

★

Disembark? Bag it? Beat it? Alley-oop?

Ah, the heck with it! The burning plane was only a few hundred feet above the ocean. *Gotta scoot! NOW!!*

Lieutenant Poppy clawed open the cockpit and clambered out. Immediately, chute and all, he was sucked into the 120-mph slipstream. He bumped down the fuselage and banged his head on the tail.

And that did it!

"BAIL OUT!" he yelled at the rapidly descending plane. "HIT THE SILK! WE'RE DITCHING!!"

J ust an hour before his date with destiny, Poppy had sat in the ready room of the *San Jac* amidst his fellow pilots. His tall, lanky frame was sprawled casually over a battered metal chair, as the aroma of steaming coffee mingled with that of a sweat-stained jumpsuit. Just twenty years old. A goddamn kid doing a man's job.

Often the victim of his mess-mates pranks, Poppy stands guard over what he thinks is a "snubnose" 120 mm deck-gun.

His merry blue eyes examined his comrades-in-arms. Gone were "Buff," "Fizz," "Moose," and "Lovecakes," the preppie monikers of his youth. To these men "breeding" was something you did with your mouth.

There was "Coalhole" Kupferberg, from the mean streets of New York. Next to him, Bud "Buttwad" Watt from Topeka. Behind Buttwad, "Lizardlips" Perelli and "Pussywipe" Piluski from Chicago. Around them a dozen other leathery, laconic airmen. Real men. They smoked. They drank. They gave whores teddy bears on shore leave.

Poppy never did any of that. But he really liked them, these common, hairy men. And in their rough way, they really liked him back. He was pretty sure of that.

He was their mascot, they said. Their fancy-pants flyboy from back East. They joshed him, they ribbed him, they gave him the merry razz. They made him chug Brasso and put tarantulas in his bed. Because he had bum luck with equipment, they nicknamed him "Hex," and threw weird finger signs at him to ward off bad luck. They laid bets on when he'd finally make it to a target. But it was all in good fun, and he took it on the jaw. It was their way of saying he was an OK kid. Affection, Navy-style.

And boy, had they had fun! One day on a routine training flight, the undercarriage on Poppy's Avenger collapsed as he was coming in. He crash-landed, totaling the big bomber. Some joker had removed a strut from his landing gear. Jeepers, what a hoot!

> **Poppy's Avenger collapsed as he was coming in. He crash-landed, totaling the big bomber. Some joker had removed a strut from his landing gear. Jeepers, what a hoot!**

Of course it wasn't all fun and games. This was war. People often died or were killed. There were too many days when the mournful sound of "Taps" would echo in the despairing emptiness of Poppy's young soul. Then he'd have a Grasshopper and feel right as rain.

It's gonna be Taps if I don't get outta this darn chute. Can't see! White and Delaney. Maybe they bailed out over the island. Hope not.

Melvin says there's a Jap commander there who cuts your nuts off with a bamboo knife and eats them raw, right in front of you!

Goshdarn, this water's cold. West's dropping a raft. Melvin's dropping the medical kit. Swell fellows. Everything's gonna be fine. Gonna be a breeze ...

OK. In the raft.

Wait! Guys! Where're they going? HELP! Don't leave me here! OH GOLLY! Gonna pop! Not here ...! Not now ...! PLEASE!

Where am I? OK—coming back now. Shot down. Keep away from island. Jap major, bamboo knife, eats nuts raw. Watch seems to've stopped. No—still going. Sun's the same...

Jeepers— Must've been out for TWENTY FOUR HOURS!!

Could eat a horse. Thirsty too. Water! Must have water! Don't drink sea ... go MAD!

★

OK.

What's that? A shark! Quick, the .38! BLAM! THERE! Darn, just a wave. NO! NO—a SHARK for sure! BLAM! No...wavesharkwaveshark

Going MAD ... delirious ... must have water soda Coke Nehi ...

Hey, BARBARA! What's that, sweetie? A martini? Whatta gal!

Straight up, with two olives, just the way ...

Hey, wait! Don't go! Bar— COME BACK! LEAVE ME THE MARTINI, AT LEAST! Oh No! GONNA POP AGAIN!

> **"Sir, we have to clear the bridge now and dive. The Japs have spotted us. Plus your raft is full of bullet holes. You coming on board or what?"**

Well, it's not, Poppy. We're actually floating on the back of a HUGE FAT JAP!!

You mean...?

YES! He's swimming to Chichi Jima to cut our nuts off with a bamboo knife and EAT THEM RAW!!

NO!!

Shut up! Don't panic! Pass me the .38.

BLAM! BLAM! BLAM! GOT HIM! HE'S A GONER! WE'RE SAFE!

OH GOD! WHAT'S THAT COMING OUT OF THE SEA? IT'S A MONSTER, POPPY!

LOOK AT ITS SNOUT!! SO LONG, POPPY, MUMSY, BAR, HERBERT!!

OK. Today's the day. Decision. Must have food. Been two days. Maybe more. Only one thing to do. Cut foot off and eat it. OK, let's go. Shoot! No knife. Get foot...to...mouth Darn it—that's hard! WHY SO TALL! Calm down ... Try again. Bite off CHUNK! AAAGGHH! That's DISGUSTING! BLEEUCCH! OH NO! PASSING OUT AGAAAIN!

Know something, Poppy? Head's much clearer today. Not so hungry, either.

You know, old thing, you're right. Not so thirsty, either. Perhaps the worst's over.

Could be. Now, Poppy, don't act surprised when I tell you this, OK?

OK, old thing.

You think this is a life raft we're on don't you?

Yes. Standard-issue yellow Navy raft ...

"Welcome aboard, sir. Name and rank, please."

"Where am I?"

"US Submarine *Finback*, sir. Sent to pick you up."

"Thank God! Almost a goner! Been in water days,—weeks, maybe. Sharks everywhere. No water, no food, no martinis, no tennis, no mayo..."

"We got the signal at 9:33 A.M., sir. It's now 11:56 A.M. You've been in the water for, er, 143 minutes. Like some lunch?"

"Wait just a darn minute! This another dumb Navy joke?"

"Sir, we have to clear the bridge now, and dive. The Japs have spotted us. Plus your raft is full of bullet holes. You coming on board or what?"

★

Like all pilots, Poppy lost a few "kites."
His daredevil, happy-go-lucky approach to
flying made him the toast of the mess.

★

Top: After Poppy's heroic crash-landing in the Pacific, his grief-stricken comrades anxiously await news of his fate.

Bottom: Navy pilots were warned about being captured by the dreaded Jap commander of Chichi Jima, Masoko Sadistikawa. For Poppy, this cemented a subconscious link between Asian features and his congenital vomiting problem.

As soon as the Prez heard of Poppy's heroism, he set the wheels in motion to reward his son's valor in the proper manner. A recommendation for DFC (Distinguished Flying Cross) was soon speeding its way toward the *San Jacinto* as Poppy had once sped toward his target on Chichi Jima.

As for Poppy, it was many weeks before he hop-scotched his way back across the Pacific theater to rejoin his squadron. No one was more surprised than the naturally modest young air-ace to find that he was now officially a war hero. In the twinkling of an eye, he had joined the illustrious brotherhood of Chuck Yaeger, Douglas Bader, and the Red Baron.

But his erstwhile buddies had changed. Gone were the practical jokes, the ribbing, the joshing, the merry razzes. The green-eyed monster of envy had entered the picture and the result was not pretty.

One night in the mess it all came to a head. "Pussywipe" Piluski, the coarsest of the crew, had been imbibing pretty heavily. Round about midnight he staggered over to where Poppy was quietly nursing a Coke.

"Say, Georgeherbertwalker," he slurred in a whiskey-sodden baritone. "Wanna ask you favor."

"That depends, Pussywipe," countered Poppy, trying to keep things jocular.

"How about your old man recommends me for a DFC?" said the inebriated oaf. "See—I took off this morning, flew a couple miles, and landed again. Pretty distinguished flying, wouldn't you say, old thing?"

Poppy started to say something sincere and generous, but the brutish sot blundered on. "And know what?" he slurred. "Didn't lose a single crewman."

This was too much for the ardent young flier. Smashing his Coke down on the mess-table, he got up. With one sweeping savage motion, he paid his check.

But the drunken Pole's sarcastic words rankled. That Christmas of 1944, Poppy confronted the Prez. He had to know. Was he a war hero? Or did DFC really stand for Dem Fancy Connections?

> ### This was too much for the ardent young flier. Smashing his Coke down on the mess-table, he got up. With one sweeping savage motion, he paid his check.

"What you have got to get through your thick skull is this," said the Prez in his firm but loving manner. "Comes the day when you have to Run Things, it won't be enough to have been an ordinary Joe. You'll have to have been a war hero."

"Yes, Papa."

"Speaking of Joe, old Joe Kennedy has been running up and down the entire East Coast telling everyone his boy Jack's a goddamn war hero, just because he got run down by a Jap and swam a few feet. Well I'll be damned if some jumped-up bog-paddy Boston bootlegger's boy is gonna be a war hero, and NOT YOU!!"

"Yes Papa." ∎

★

Boyz in the Hoodz: the 1946 Skull and Bones Admissions Committee

★

Chapter 4

Skulls and Boners

O N AUGUST 15 1945, V-J Day, Japan's vile hegemony was forever crushed. The war was over. Poppy and his new bride, the blushing, demure, dew-fresh twenty-year-old former Barbara Pierce, were posted in Virginia Beach when they heard the news. Like all Americans, they were thrilled to bits. But before they joined their friends to crack a few Cokes, they had an important date. They sought out their favorite Episcopal Church, Holy Trinity, and went down on their knees to give thanks for this great victory to the Holy Trinity: God the Father, God the Son, and God the Holy Spirit (known to Episcopalians as God Sr., God Jr., and God III).

The call to prayer was not a spur-of-the-moment impulse. Poppy was acting on a gentlemanly principle drummed into him by his father from his earliest years: First God, then the drinks.

That fall it was off to Yale on the GI Bill. Of course most people at Yale, including Poppy, didn't need to go on the GI Bill. But Poppy had earnt that right in the crucible of war, and using it was a badge of honor. Besides, the Prez's allowance barely kept them in canapés.

Poppy to chose what was for someone of his background an unconventional major—economics—and an even more unconventional minor, voodoo.

Y ou are the seed of mighty knights. "Back through tunnel of history goes this seed, back through the Masons and the Rosicrucians, through centuries of fire and blood, to the Temple Mount of Jerusalem in the year 1118 A.D. In that holy place was founded the mighty Order of Knights Templar, fierce warrior-monks, mystic knights clad in white and splayed red cross. You will be the vanguard of the

★

Crusades, the shadow rulers of the known world, the keepers of Christianity's most sacred secrets."

Far below the Skull and Bones' fearsome structure on High Street, in a secret basement under the notorious "secret" basement, under the actual basement, Poppy knelt before seven robed figures, two of whom would one day be Secretary of Agriculture.

Above his head was the flickering light of black candles, hanging from a low vaulted ceiling that teemed with carvings of demonic gargoyles and arcane symbols. He was being initiated as a "Skull"—the inner circle of Skull and Bones, superior to "Bones" or "Bonesmen." The latter were straightforward run-of-the-mill members who didn't even know there was a difference between them and "Skulls."

So he was a knight now, thought Poppy. Wow! Some challenge. He couldn't just coast through life. He'd have to fight duels with other knights, rescue maidens, slay dragons and whatnot on a daily basis. But at the end of his knightly quest would be the Holy Grail of Running Things.

"Here is the awful history of our secret society's symbol. Hear well, O Novice Bush, and feel the dread in your bones."

Another robed figure was speaking. He would one day make his fortune by cornering the market in sorghum.

"There was a knight who loved a lady. But alas she died. Distraught with grief, he went privily by night to her grave. He disinterred the beauti-

The Civil War section of S&B's fabled bone collection. The club's unofficial slogan in Poppy's freshman year was: "Cut classes! Raise glasses! Play ball with the dead of Manassas!"

★

ful corpse and consummated his love for her.

"Nine months later, he was summoned from his castle by a phantom voice. A child had been born to his paramour. He returned to the grave to find there his newborn son: a skull and two leg bones."

Phew! Spooky! Poppy wasn't sure about the X-rated part, of course, but what a yarn!

The Ceremony was reaching its climax. The seven robed figures formed a circle round Poppy. He pricked his finger with an ornate dagger. He exchanged blood with all seven men.

Then he was given a secret decoder ring, and taught the secret Skull handshake. Finally, under pain of death, he was told the society's darkest secrets, secrets so secret they cannot even be revealed in these uncensored pages. Things like what the eye on a dollar bill means, where Judge Crater is buried, and the contents of the Fatima letter.

A s he had been at Andover and in the Navy, Poppy was in great demand at Yale. Like all peppy undergrads he neglected his studies. (This was no problem, since by a clandestine arrangement with the faculty, Skulls were guaranteed straight A's).

But he had to maintain his reputation as an legendary all-round athlete, and he flung himself into the fray. He garnered major letters in fifteen sports and minor ones in twenty-six others. On one occasion he played Harvard simultaneously at baseball, basketball, squash, and tennis. And won!

Then there was George Jr. In July 1946 a beautiful bouncing baby boy was born to Bar. Unlike other men of his day, Poppy pitched in with the parenting. For example, he occasionally held the baby for Bar, and he packed away all the gifts from Tiffany's in their little blue boxes.

But it was at Skull and Bones that his mettle was being tried. And nothing tested him more than helping to organize the highpoint of the Skull and Bones year: its annual Halloween party.

Radicals have often demanded that Skull and Bones should be closed because of its restricted admissions policy. According to these busybodies, no blacks or women have ever been allowed through its doors.

Nothing could be further from the truth. Blacks have been allowed into S&B for as long as there have been lavish feasts to be cleaned up. True, in the early years of the century, their tongues were often surgically removed to prevent disclosure of club secrets. However, by Poppy's day this deterrent was far more humane, having been reduced to the mere threat of life imprisonment.

And Skull and Bones has always admitted women—provided they were midgets.

The midgets were Poppy's job. He had to arrange transportation from various parts of the globe for some two dozen of them. The club had regular suppliers, mostly in Europe and Latin America. No-one would tell him what the midgets did, other than they were the club's traditional Halloween hostesses, and that the services they provided gave new meaning to the terms

★

"Skull" and "Bones."

Poppy turned the arduous job to positive effect. He made many interesting contacts. One young street hustler from Panama City furnished a grateful Poppy with no less than three

ALL MEMBERS AND GUESTS

(NO WOMEN, JEWS OR COLORED)
LIBRARY, BANQUET ROOMS

GROUND LEVEL

ALL MEMBERS —
SOME ('PREFERED) GUESTS

SKELETON
CLOSET

BONE
ROOM

BASEMENT TROPHY ROOM

ALL MEMBERS, SOME
COLORED, (SERVANTS)

PRIVATE
"TASTING"
ROOMS

BEER
100K

WINE CELLARS

D & I
ROOMS

(DISCIPLINE
&
INITIATION)

SENIOR MEMBERS
(BONES & SKULLS)
SOME WOMEN,
(SEE TEXT)

D & I
ROOMS

(DISCIPLINE
&
INITIATION)

"SECRET" BASEMENT

SKULLS ONLY (NO BONES)

SECRET
BAR

P R I V A T E

C l u B I c L I e s

STEAM
ROOM

ACTUAL SECRET BASEMENT

TREASURER +
GUESTS ONLY

CRYPT

VAULT

TOP SKULLS ONLY

ALTAR

BULLION, SECURITIES,
JEWELRY, PETTY CASH,
WEAPONS

SECRET
CRYPT

NO ONE
ADMITTED
EVER

MAUSOLEUM

ALL MEMBERS
(DECEASED)

S&B's ultra-secret lower levels, published for the first time here. According to S&B tradition anyone who knows of, or even reads about, this secret, is marked for death.

delightful little women for the 1947 festivities. The hustler's name? Manuel Noriega.

By Halloween night, Poppy had surpassed himself. It looked to be the best Halloween bash in history, and most of the credit went to Poppy. Then two of the senior (Top) Skulls dropped a bombshell. Poppy's last duty was to fetch the traditional Guest of Honor.

She was ready and waiting for him, they said. All he had to do was pick her up from the New Haven City Morgue.

Some literal-minded readers might find taking a naked cadaver from a morgue—in this case an attractive blonde in her mid-twenties—morally questionable. However, these were young men of excellent background who were observing a time-honored tradition. Hindsight has no place calling into question their good judgment. And from a purely legal point of view, the lady had not withheld her consent.

For Poppy, the situation was clear. This was a test—his toughest yet. He had to rise to the occasion. Quickly he ripped off his Lillian Hellman costume—leaving himself only the garter-belt and the overcoat—and got the Guest of Honor dressed.

He decided the best way to divert attention from the deceased nature of his "date" would be to pretend they were both drunk. He got one of her

★

arms round his neck, put one of his round her waist, and wove out of the morgue. He recalls this as being less difficult than it sounds, except for "the whole lolling-tongue thing."

Slapping his "friend" occasionally to "bring her around" and singing "When the Saints Come Marching In" at the top of his lungs, he weaved to the corner of York Street and tried to hail a cab.

At this point he was accosted by an eight-year-old boy dressed as a pumpkin.

"Hey mister, trick or treat!"

"Go away please, for goshsake! I'm sick! I mean we're drunk! Cab! Jeepers why won't they stop?"

"Hey lady, gimme some candy or I'll squirt you!"

"She doesn't have any candy. She's drunk, OK?"

Poppy began staggering away from the boy, who, naturally, followed him.

"What's wrong with your girlfriend? Is she dead? She looks dead!"

"No. We're squiffy, you see? Polluted! Absolutely stinko! Please leave us alone! I beseech you!"

"Is she stiff yet? Can I feel her? I wanna feel her! Let me feel her!!"

The child grabbed the blonde's leg and Poppy lost his balance. He and the blonde fell to the pavement. Poppy's raincoat fell open, revealing his garter-belt.

"Eeeuuw! A sex fiend!"

A woman weighing well over two hundred pounds now appeared. Poppy tried to hike the blonde up in a fireman's lift.

"Hey Mom!" screeched the boy. "There's one of those decadent bourgeois sex fiends here you told

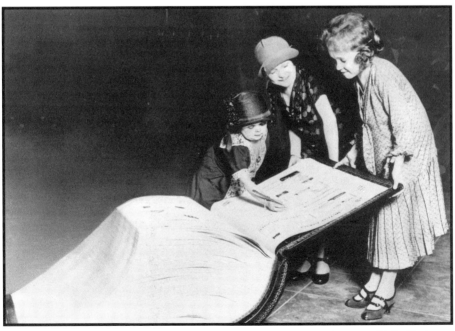

The "little women"—midget hostesses of S&B's notorious Halloween Night Party, sign the club's guest book.

★

In a nostalgic visit to Skull and Bones, Poppy shows Bar the crypt where he once spent the night in a sarcophagus full of raw eggs and garter snakes.

me about. He's got a dead lady with him!"

The mother bore down on them.

"What are you doing to my baby, you filth?"

"Nothing! I—er—he—er—"

Poppy got the blonde on his shoulders, but his raincoat fell open again. The woman began hitting him with a huge handbag.

"You stinking capitalist jackal!" she yelled. "These gutters will run red with your blood!!"

Poppy threw all caution to the winds and ran. It was a full half-mile to Bones, and he had a 120-pound handicap, but he made it in four minutes. Needless to say, the Top Skulls had had him tracked every moment of his ordeal, and the group was regaled with tales of his antics. But he'd come through like a true Top Skull—not to mention ensuring the attendance of the Guest of Honor.

He was the toast of the evening—as was she. (And he found out what the midgets did, too.)

Over the rest of the celebration, we draw a discreet veil, save only for one small but highly significant encounter.

Toward the end of the evening, Poppy, now a Top Skull-elect, was approached by a man in leather mask, dressed as a cardinal. He seemed older than the undergrads, a visitor from New York. He had a vulgar bog-paddy accent and had trouble pronouncing his R's.

He said he and some friends were putting together a group to implement the National Security Act. It would be select, discreet, not unlike Skull and Bones, and would play a huge role in America's future. He'd like Poppy to consider joining them. He had a soft spot for Navy men from Yale, he said. He left his card.

William Casey had entered Poppy's life.   ∎

★

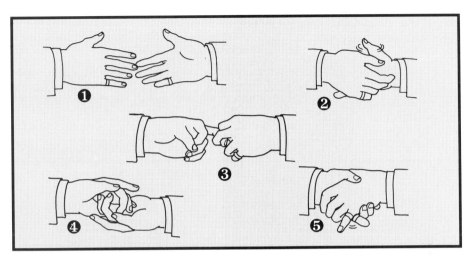

Sequence of the secret S&B handshake.

Poppy shares the secret Skull and Bones handshake with the alumni of other death's-head secret societies around the world. Such men form a worldwide brotherhood of those Born to Run Things that cuts across all political lines. Bottom right: Poppy is delighted to discover that the S & B handshake is the same as the SS secret handshake.

Election Day 1967: would-be Congressman George Herbert Walker Bush greets voters at a Houston polling center for some last-minute campaigning.

★

Chapter 5

Oil Wells That End Well

AT ANDOVER, where other boys idolized "Red" Grange, or Herbert Hoover, Poppy's hero had always been Tom Mix. Had they known this, his Eastern friends and relatives might have been a tad less perplexed when Poppy moved his family in 1950 to the apparently quite ghastly West Texas town of Odessa.

Texas! Where men were men and shot one another before breakfast. Where women wore pearls the size of golfballs and cars had antlers. Where no one would make fun of you if you wanted to wear those nifty boots with pointy toes and spangly stuff all over them.

Of course Odessa was a hick town in the boonies. You couldn't buy a pair of Topsiders for love or money. Odessans thought squash was something you did to fruit. Or—if they knew item one about sports—it was something that "fruits" did.

But they did have oil. Boy, did they have oil! Buckets of the stuff! Squirting up all over the place. All you had to do was rent one of these rig thingummies, plonk it down in a field, and boom! You could make a fortune.

Some investment was needed—for the rig thingummies and for the field. Say half a million dollars, (in 1992 terms a paltry ten or twelve million).

Though Poppy was wild and free and independent, he decided to let his father in on the action. In 1953 he borrowed half a mill from the Prez, and wouldn't you know, hit oil the first time out! He had some later setbacks—for instance, an offshore rig he owned caught fire, and as the locals put it, "boiled half the goddam shrimp in the Gulf."

Over the years, though, displaying the same innate business acumen and careful stewardship he later brought to the nation's economy,

★

Poppy and fellow CIA operatives in Dallas react to Warren Commision's finding that Oswald acted alone. *At center:* **Lee Harvey Oswald's step-brother Pee Wee Harvey Oswald.**

Poppy returned to the Prez several thousand dollars on his investment.

But as always with Poppy, money didn't matter. What mattered was Texas. Texas was so big-hearted! So open! So unselfconscious! So American! Such a great place to bring up kids. Soon Poppy and Bar were Papa and Mumsy to a fine family of four strapping Texans and a girl.

(Though unfortunately one of the boys, Neil, was diagnosed in childhood as suffering from a rare form of dyslexia which made it impossible for him to read zeroes.)

Within just a few years, Poppy fit right in, a Texan with the best of 'em, in his wide-brim Stetson and his nifty boots with pointy toes and spangly stuff. Why, he stood about as tall as a ten-foot jackrabbit!

Some things, natch, the greenhorn got wrong. For the longest time he thought Tony Lamas were made of llamas and grits was stuff you put on roads in winter. Then there was

another teensy blindspot that always riled him: the proper pronunciation of "oil business."

In their gruff, untutored way, Texans pronounce this "oil bidniz." For some reason this was beyond Poppy. The closest he ever got was "bidnid." More often it was " b i z n i d . " Or—worse still— "didnid."

Unlike the East, where people were more self-conscious and picky, Texans didn't care about such silly little gaffes. They just slapped your back and squeezed off a coupla rounds at your feet, and that was that.

Which made it all the more galling, when Poppy finally decided to throw his wide-brim Stetson into the ring and run for office, to find that Texan politics weren't a bit like Texans.

His first time out, in 1964, against a dangerous left-wing radical called Ralph Yarborough, was a nightmare. Even though he'd lived in Texas for years and had not just one, but six pairs of nifty boots with pointy toes, Yarborough called him a "carpetbagger!" Ouch!

So he lost. So he became a state-wide political joke. Ask him if he gave a hoot. What Yarborough didn't know—what no one knew, not even Bar—was that he had another string to his bow.

From the moment he set foot in Texas, Poppy had been CIA. Yup, he'd done it. He'd come through for Casey. For all these years, he'd led a double life. One as a tough but loving father, successful executive in the oil bidnid, and statewide political joke. The other as the eyes and ears of the Company in the gas-station of democracy.

Whenever a Texan heart thrilled to those stirring words, "The eyes of Texas are upon you," Poppy could safely say that two of them were his.

Ironically, the CIA was the whole reason Poppy was in Texas. When he joined the CIA in 1948, he requested a posting right to the heart of the enemy, Russia. He suggested the beautiful old port of Odessa in the Ukraine, because the Black Sea offered tip-top sailing.

Alas, these were early days at the CIA. There was much internal disorganization. Many divisions didn't even have maps of the countries they were supposed to be spying on. In short, no one at CIA knew where Odessa was.

One goof led to another, and before he knew it, Poppy found himself in West Texas in a covert CIA operation called SPAIDS (Semi-Public Assets—Illegal Domestic Surveillance).

Casey was tremendously busy at the time, using his cover as Wall Street hustler to plant spies in the Kremlin, terminate Red collaborators in Europe, and root out homosexuals from the British Secret Service. By

★

the time Poppy got through to him and explained the goof, it was too late.

Against all Company directives, SPAIDS Op 48/WT/GB, codename "Tinkerbell," kept a personal journal of his activities. The following excerpts chronicle the drudgery, the setbacks, the frustration, and the unexpected rewards of being a "secret agent man."

July 5, 1958 (Midland, Texas). JACKPOT! WOWEE! Journalist in town. Claims British but Jew name. Positive no Jews in UK. (MEMO: Check at John Birch meet this eve.) Paper something called *Financial Times*. Looks legit, but printed on PINK PAPER!

The horse's mouth: Tycoon Poppy learns first-hand from a Texas roughneck the difference between a Hughes International No. 7 cold-forged tungsten-tip drill-bit and "that twirly thingumajig."

MORE CLUES: At drinks wanted VODKA! Says story on LABOR angle of oil boom ! Made weird joke (?) about ironic Odessa USA being on a "BLACK SEA of oil."

CONCLUSION: Crazy hunch this individ. is KGB. Poss. trying to DEFECT (?!?!) Could be big feather cap.

ACTION TAKEN: Detailed report by phone to Langley. (Whoops! Still, who's gonna read this?) Disappointing response. Low-level op on switchboard unimpressed (amused?).

July 6–18: Repeated calls to Casey. No dice. Out to lunch first three, out of town second three, out of country all the rest.

July 23: KGB op left town. On BUS! Shoot!!! One that GOT AWAY!

Jan. 5 1959: Top-secret gen. memo from DCI. Wow! Delivered U.S. MAIL—BRILLIANT! As per textbook - no concealment best concealment. (NB for future.)

Directive indicates grave prob. use personal phones to contact HQ.

★

App. Russkies a. are tapping many ops. b. have technology to deliver massive nuke "zaps" down phone lines! (BASTARDS!)

R/kies identify agent by destination of phone call, instantly trace origin, then blow op (and phone) to happy hunting grounds! (DIRTY ROTTEN BASTARDS!)

DCI says US has same techno, but no defense as yet.

NEW RULE: Pay phones only, NEVER COLLECT. (SHOULD THINK NOT!!!)

Nov. 20, 1963: Received package from Corpus Christi via airfreight as per directive. (Long flat heavy.)

As profits poured in from Zapata Oil, Poppy splurged on a new sofa for his burgeoning brood.

A/P/D drove Dallas to deliver to op in sleazy nightclub (the Carousel). Vulgar lout, Jack something.

Asked what package was said none of my f-wording beeswax. Was for transshipment to another op and keep my f-wording preppie mouth shut or I'd be ICED! (?) REALLY!! People Company hiring these days! YUKKO!

Nov. 25: Whole JFK thing weirder and weirder. (Blessing in disguise, but pretty blatant of commies if you ask this op. BASTARDS!)

Anyhow, here's Jack-something blasting Oswald on TV. WHAT GIVES?

New Company termination poli-

cy? Best-concealment-no-concealment? Color me BAFFLED!!!

Nov. 26: Called Langley (from pay-phone!) for clarification re JFK-Oswald-Jack-something biz. Spoke to assistant Ee-howard (?) Hunt. Listened carefully to clarification request. (Good man!) Told me to hold while checked.

Had to move car (blocking delivery to chili joint). Next second PAY-PHONE BLOWS SKY-HIGH!!! (BASTARDS!! LOUSY STINKING BASTARDS!!)

May 1 1966: Campaign timeout. In Dallas on oil bidnid (??? biznid? The heck with it). Realized

BEING FOLLOWED!

Ran tail to ground in chi-chi bar at Adolphus Hotel. Stunning blonde . (!) Local girl. Also CIA doing "intra-agency security check." (Sfunny Langley didn't mention anything.)

Codename "Yellow Rose." (LIKE THAT!!!)

Ran "quiz" on routine covert stuff, e.g. codenames and locations of other ops in Dallas–Fort Worth–Abilene area. Also h/classified early–warning stuff at Rattlesnake AFB. App. yours truly came through flying colors. (YOU BETCHA!!)

One thing (OK, drink) led to another, and Bob's-your-uncle we're upstairs in her room, pitching MUCHO WOO! I mean THE MOST FANTASTIC STUN-NING, SUPERBO, YOU-KNOW-WHAT IN THE HISTORY OF Y O U - K N O W - WHAT!!!

May 2: Something terrible and wonderful has happened. This op's IN LOVE!! The birds are singing sweeter, the trees are looking greener, my serve's improved 1000%!

Meeting again Dallas next week. CAN'T WAIT! No calls. But wish I COULD! OH, WOW!

MEMO TO SELF: Bring all DCI directives from last five years for Yellow Rose (SOARING VIOLINS!!) to shred. (Part of new internal security measures).

I n 1967 the civilized forward-looking voters of Houston's "Silk-stocking" Seventh District provided Poppy with a stepping stone to his true home, Washington, D.C. For the moment, his involvment with the CIA waned as he explored other corridors and closets of power. This spy was coming in from the cold.

Poppy had one last brush with "democracy." In 1970 the Prez per-

A rare photograph of Congressman Bush with fellow CIA operative (codename "Yellow Rose").

suaded him to run for Senate against Lloyd Bentsen. This was Poppy's big chance, said the Prez. The long nightmare of Soviet-style welfare statism was ending. The Republican Renaissance was peeking over the horizon. With both the Kennedy boys dead—and good riddance—the nation was looking for a new political dynasty. Why not the Bushes? Poppy was a damn sight better-looking than that drunken bog-paddy Teddy.

Poppy charged into the campaign like a mad thing. And ran slap-bang into the same kind of verminous assaults he had six years earlier. Lloyd Bentsen renewed all the dumb accusations of "carpetbagging." He let no opportunity pass to suggest that Poppy's fresh-faced openness, lanky elegance, and attractive light tenor speaking voice were conclusive evidence of homosexuality

On one occasion at the Press Club in Dallas, when Poppy mentioned JFK, Bentsen said "Congressman, I worked with Jack Kennedy. I knew Jack Kennedy. And Congressman, you're no Jack Kennedy."

It was despicable. But it worked.

The night of the election, Poppy sat with the Prez as the returns came in. As it became clear that Bentsen foul tactics had paid off, the Prez's face became grimmer and grimmer. Poppy could almost see the sand of his hopes and dreams trickling out the hourglass of his soul into the desert of history. And as he conceded defeat a few hours later, he knew that a long night lay ahead of him.

The Prez still knew how to make that Brooks Brothers belt buckle bite! OUCH! ■

Poppy and his Papa Prescott watch him lose his second Senate race (to Lloyd Bentsen in 1970). Seconds later the elder Bush took off his belt and administered the usual punishment.

★

Part of Richard Nixon's training of his favorite protégé was to have him assume various subservient roles. In this official 1971 White House portrait, Poppy appears as the legendary butler Arthur Treacher.

★

Chapter 6

U.N. Interlude
Debacle on 43rd Street

THE WHITE HOUSE. A balmy late afternoon in the summer of 1971. The President's private quarters. The temperature outside is in the 80s, but merry flames flicker brightly in the grate. To keep the room cool and balmy, the powerful air-conditioning is turned all the way up. Just the way President Richard Nixon likes it. He sinks contentedly back into his favorite leather armchair. His feet rest comfortably on his inert wife Pat.

Nixon's ambassador to the U.N. is down from New York for a briefing on the crucial dual-representation-of-China issue. Mr. Ambassador is currently serving the President martinis from a silver tray. He is dressed in a white mess-jacket, white tie, and white cotton gloves. He wears a wig of tight white curls. He is in black-face.

This week Poppy Bush is Rochester from the old *Jack Benny Show*.

Last week he was Arthur Treacher, the indomitable butler of countless '30s comedies. The visit before that, he portrayed Jeeves the immortal gentleman's gentleman created by P.G. Wodehouse.

The legacy Richard Nixon has bequeathed to the history books is that of a towering statesman whose political intuition was second to none and whose unblinking eagle eye out-foxed the Russian bear.

The thing Poppy remembers best about him is what a hoot he could be.

For the dynamic young Republican up-and-comer, the Nixon White House was a place of sun and fun. The President calling Brezhnev on the hot line, making chicken noises, and hanging up. The President and Bebe Rebozo seeing who could do the longest belch. The President telling Julie that he got the idea for the SST from David Eisenhower's ears.

Even now, he was throwing the martini—glass, olive, and all—into the fireplace. In his Jack Benny voice, he ordered Rochester to go back to the sideboard and start all over again, with even less (expletive deleted) vermouth.

But there was a purpose to what Texans like Poppy called "funnin'."

★

The President was testing him, with these kooky routines. They were always the same: he had to be the underdog and Nixon in charge. So they were also a lesson in how power works. How far was Poppy willing to go? A British accent? Blackface? A French maid's outfit?

Nixon once said, "The best lunch to pack for the long journey to the top is crow pie." It was a bit like that thing LBJ said the time he went to visit him at his ranch.

"George," said the wily old blackguard, "I like to remind boys getting into politics that you gotta eat a peck o' dirt afore you die. With you, George, I'd make that two."

Peck of dirt, crow pie, mused Poppy as he waved the vermouth bottle at the gin. If it got him this close to the action without all the muss and fuss of elections, heck, he'd eat owl-poop.

"Hey Tinkerbell!" boomed a loud Maryland voice. "Who you supposed to be today? Coretta King?"

Poppy admired Agnew immensely. He was crude and boorish, but straightforward and honest. Someone had told him that Agnew was worried about being on the '72 ticket and regarded every male Republican in D.C. as a rival, including Poppy. He even suspected that poor deformed Eisenhower boy.

Poppy felt Nixon was masterly for choosing Agnew. Picking a man cruder and not so bright as you for Veep was clever. It made you look that much smoother and smarter. Something worth remembering.

"How's those blue-assed baboons up in the Jew-En, Tinker baby? You pull them bones outa their noses and shove 'em up their

Poppy's unfortunate habit of "popping"—vomiting unexpectedly in public—has plagued him throughout a long and distinguished career. Over time he has developed various techniques for disguising an inadvertent "pop" The condition is exacerbated by the presence of Asians, which proved particularly embarrassing when Poppy was Envoy to China. At their regular weekly meetings, Premier Deng thoughtfully provided Poppy with a "popping pot"

★

The President of the United States being ignored by two Arabs.

The President reveals his plan to give the unborn fetus "a means to fight back"

The President fondles a small mammal presented to him by actor Richard Gere.

★

The President helps Senator Jesse Helms to walk erect.

The President meeting with every black Republican in America

★

Above: The President welcomes two white Haitians to the United States

Left: The President, having discovered a loaded handgun on his person, wrestles himself to the ground, and subdues himself.

★

Poppy Bush and Jimmy Carter discuss one-term presidencies.

The President "scores" his weekly Halcion prescription

★

ass, OK?"

Agnew's job was insulting people. It was a dirty job, but someone had to do it. What with the Commies at the very gates and all. He was pretty good at it, too. Especially when he got rolling with those great alliterative things Bill Safire and Pat Buchanan wrote.

Golly, here were Bill and Pat now. And him still in blackface, darn it!

"How about 'the sibilant sycophants of Sisyphean socialism'?"

"Get off the classics kick, Pat. It underlines the paucity of a Georgetown education."

"What's a paucity?"

"Well, Newark, for one."

"I don't get it."

"Precisely. How about 'the mildewed milquetoasts of menopausal Marxism'?"

"What is it with you and menopause?"

"What is it with you and sibilance?"

Pretty soon they'd get on one of their Nazi-Jew routines—Hitler had a point, Israel needs nukes, and so on. An absolute riot back and forth, like ping-pong. The Pat and Bill Show. Quite challenging too, because Safire in particular knew scads of those words you challenge at Scrabble.

But no Pat and Bill Show today. More people were arriving. All those

> **...More people were arriving. All those simply brilliant guys with German names: Haldeman, Erlichman, Kleindeinst, Krogh, Magruder, Ziegler. The Boys in the Bund, Safire called them, which always got Pat sore...**

simply brilliant guys with German names: Haldeman, Erlichman, Kleindienst, Krogh, Magruder, Ziegler. The Boys in the Bund, Safire called them, which always got Pat sore, because he said the Bund had never gotten a fair shake. Then Safire would say that wasn't the point and Pat oughta spend more time going to the theater. Pretty soon it'd be back to the Kraut-this and Kike-that stuff. Hilarious.

Here was John Mitchell looking pleased as punch. Must have found another of his "typos" in the Bill of Rights. And Martha with her skirt hiked up round the hipflask in her pantyhose.

And—cheese and crackers!—here's Rebozo the Clown swanning in as usual, like he owns the place. Probably does. Sure enough, he shifts Nixon's feet over and sits alongside them on Pat.

No-one talked to Poppy. (Except for Martha, who addressed him as "boy" and tried to get him to make her an old-fashioned.)

The President tells the gang to listen up. Especially George. Everyone turns to look at Poppy. (Actually quite a few look around or behind him. Goshdarn it! He doesn't look that much like Rochester!)

Kissinger comes on the TV. Silence. No one wants to say anything, because Kissinger has mikes everywhere. A nifty-looking Asian girl in not too many clothes—must be one of Herr Doktor's secretaries—appears near the bottom of the screen. She smiles nervously, like, "Are we finished dictation?" Kissinger shoves her off-screen.

"Greetings from Beijing. That's Peking to you, Spiro."

"Yeah? I'll take the pork lo mein and cold sesame noodles."

Only Bebe Rebozo laughs. Nixon rumples his hair affectionately.

Poppy is—what's the word?—nonplussed. All summer long he's been tearing round New York trying to get enough U.N. votes for the American dual-representation proposal. This would allow Red China in, without expelling tiny embattled Taiwan, Firehouse of Freedom, Doorway to Democracy, Eagle's Nest of Free Enterprise.

And now here's Hank in the lair of the enemy. Doing his version of Jane-in-Hanoi. What's the scoop?

"The initiative has been an unqvalified triumph. Ve met personally mit der Chairman, und he endorses the opening."

Everyone claps politely at the screen. Even Martha. The whole place seems to know about this thing, except the one person it affects directly, him, Poppy, the U.N. ambassador. Agitated, he drops the tray of martinis. Kissinger locates him.

"Ach, George. There you are. Cute get-up. Who you supposed to be dis week: Coretta King?"

"No suh, Mass' Kissinger I sho ... I mean, no, goshdarn it, I'm, er—"

"Bush, you vill proceed exactly as you haf been. Campaign wigorously for dual rep. Ve vill lose. Taiwan gets der boot. Den... the mas-

ter-stroke! The President will announce a trip to China! A historic opening of East and West. In one move, we have the Soviets surrounded and Hanoi's balls in der meatgrinder!"

"B-b-but then why can't I just recognize Red China?"

"Because I will not desert tiny embattled Taiwan," intoned Nixon in his beautiful speaking voice, as if he were already addressing the '72 convention. "Nor will I be dictated to by the U.N."

"Buncha slopes and boogies," added Agnew helpfully.

"Going to China means ten million votes for me," said Nixon, "and for you George, in the most important vote of you U.N. career, utter humiliation."

And utter humiliation it was. October 25, 1971, the U.N. voted to expel Taiwan. Many delegates Poppy had arduously lined up reneged at the last moment. When the vote was announced, the General Assembly went bananas. For the first time in its history, delegates openly jeered the U.S. Ambassador. Dancing erupted in the aisles.

But as he escorted the Taiwanese delegation out of the U.N., pretending to squeeze a few tears down his cheeks, in his heart Poppy was jeering back.

He had a secret. His leader, his idol, his mentor, Richard Nixon, would soon make fools of them all. This was power the way it should be. The way he liked it.

He was the most unpopular man in America that day, and it was the happiest moment of his life. ∎

As Chairman of the Republican National Committee, Poppy did his utmost to give his Party a youthful, "groovy" image.

★

Chapter 7

Chairman Wow!

I N NOVEMBER 1972, RICHARD NIXON scored a massive landslide over the radic-lib bleeding heart George McGovern. A few weeks later far-left journalist and Red-diaper baby Carl Bernstein had a meeting with his dupe Bob Woodward. Not surprisingly this occurred on Christmas day, a feast Bernstein does not celebrate.

The two decided to accomplish by foul means what they had been unable to get by fair: the defeat and disgrace of Richard Nixon. They would blow up out of all proportion some harmless campaign high jinks at the Watergate in Washington, D.C., the previous summer. Using this pretext, they would pry into the President's personal affairs and bribe his loyal cohorts with offers of sex, money, and shortened jail terms.

Woodward and Bernstein succeeded in their filthy stratagem. A great President was assassinated by their lies and distortions. The American people were denied for almost a decade the glories and benefits of the Republican renaissance.

It was like shooting Michelangelo as he painted the Sistine Chapel ceiling, or poking holes in Mozart's ear-drums, or cutting off Michael Jackson's hand before he'd donned his lengendary glove.

But what of Poppy Bush, who stood by his idol and mentor till the bitter end?

Right after the Republican triumph, the President invited his U.N. Ambassador to become the ultimate insider—Chairman of the Republican National Committee.

But then, as Watergate unfolded, each week brought new allegations, new denials from the President, new expressions of support from the Chairman of the RNC, then proof of the original allegations.

To some it might seem as though

Nixon was using the prestige of the RNC to save his skin. Poppy feels this is not the case. It is his conviction that as the infernal purposes of Bernstein and his sidekick became clear, Nixon made a fateful decision.

He would selflessly embrace the role of "bad guy" to make Poppy look that much better. If he couldn't save himself at least he would save his protégé. The President became, as it were, the Jap gunner to Poppy's soaring—and ultimately triumphant—Avenger.

"If Richard Nixon had not, in his boundless generosity with no thought of self, betrayed me at every step of Watergate," Poppy now says, "I wouldn't be the man I am today."

Soon the tragedy reached its diabolical climax and a great statesman was on his way to San Clemente and phlebitis.

But throughout the long nightmare of Watergate, Poppy was not simply doing "rope-a-dope," as another great American, soon to become a vegetable, was wont to put it. He set out to do nothing less than rejuvenate his demoralized Party.

For example, he replaced old tired staffers with young "hepcats," many of them recommended by Yellow Rose. (These young people responded in kind to his energy and enthusiasm by nicknaming him

Christmas 1975: Poppy and Bar thank President Ford for his lovely and unusual gift.

★

"Chairman Wow!")

But his boldest move was a famous Memo to State Chairmen dated January 1, 1974:

TO: ALL STATE PARTY CHAIRS
FROM: CHAIRMAN RNC
RE: "GROOVY" NEW GOP

Hey, all you "heads" out there! It's good to be "rapping" with you.

Ya know, over the last six months the Bad Guys have been laying some pretty "heavy vibes" on us Good Guys. These dudes have been claiming that the GOP is old and tired and corrupt. We all know that's a buncha owl-poop! But how do we "turn America's head around"?

Simple. We get "WITH IT"! We need a GO-GO GOP! We gotta get off Watergate and onto waterbeds! As Dylan Thomas puts it, "The times they are changing."

A. FASHION. It's time to "get down" with some of the "dynamite" new "threads":

1. Elephant bells. If anyone should be wearing these "outasite" pants, it's Republicans!

2. Tank Tops. Tailormade for advocates of a strong defense posture!

3. Chunky Soles and Heels. For Convention '76, let's see all delegates in Republican Party Platform Shoes! Let's STAND TALL again!

(PERSONAL NOTE: In his own nifty eight-inch heel New-York-Dolls- style alligator boots, your Chairman stands almost SEVEN FEET TALL!)

B. MUSIC. Hey man no need to be "bummed out" by all that rock-for-peace stuff. Dig this:

1. My boys Georgie and Jebbie listen to bands with patriotic defense-oriented names like "WAR," "BLOOD SWEAT AND TEARS," and "SOPWITH CAMEL." Let's get with it and book these dudes for Rep. Party functions. (NB: also check out "AEROSMITH"—about as close to "Aerospace" as you can get!)

2. Gal out there in rock-and-roll land called Rita Coolidge. Rare name. Perhaps related to Cool Cal.

3. Is Barry White white? Check out. We could use a Republican "Love Machine."

4. Let's get friendly record co. e.g. RCA to do "white" versions of rock classics. How 'bout "A Walk on the White Side" or "White Thing (You make my Heart Sing)"?

5. Your Chairman has created with George Jr. and Jebbie a sizzling three-man disco group. Yours truly takes top part exploiting naturally high high tenor voice. Name of "group"—THE GEE-BEES! (Please find enclosed w/ this memo, copy of Gee-Bees "Stayin' Alive"—the GOP theme song for the '70s!)

C. THE BIG ONE ... SEX!! Hey, white Republican bro, I know! It's disgusting, but we gotta have some! Sex sucks but without it we'll never be a Suc-cess!

> **Your Chairman has created with George Jr. and Jebbie, a sizzling three-man disco group. Yours truly takes top part exploiting naturally high tenor voice. Name of "group"–THE GEE-BEES!**

★

Poppy discusses various aspects of Repubican Sex with state Party chairpersons.

Your Chairman has compiled *The Republican Sex Manual.*

The *RSM* is a clear, clean, crisp, cheerful, aggressive, and well-turned-out handbook that explains in no more detail than necessary every aspect of the whole icky business. It concentrates on How Much to Wear, Disposal of Sex-Related Gunk, Sex and Taxes, and How Seldom.

My manual takes the Republican approach to S-E-X. It aims to:

a. Reduce Inflation, b. Drastically lower interest levels, and c. Protect the privates sector.

YES, VIRGINIA, there is a Sex Gap. (As a matter of fact especially in Virginia.)

While Reps were busy trying to save republic, Dems dove headlong into sex. Now they are WAY ahead!

REMEMBER: WHILE REPUB- LICANS PANT TO TAKE OVER YOUR MIND, DEMOCRATS MIND ONLY ABOUT TAKING OVER YOUR PANTS.

The *Republican Sex Manual* (see pages 61-63) was dubbed by his devoted young staff The Little Bed Book of Chairman Wow! Many of them offered help with researching the project. Poppy accepted the better-looking of these offers and invested many interesting and tiring hours on behalf of his beloved Party.

Due to envy and inertia, the RSM was repudiated by most state chairmen but snapped up by the rank and file. It became the best-kept secret of '70s Republicanism. It changed Republicans forever. Before it, the image of a Republican womanhood was a corseted sack of suet with

★

the sex appeal of a Barcalounger. Republican manhood was a stringy clam in wire-rim glasses who got his kicks imagining large missiles entering Russian silos.

Voters had never had a problem with Republican policies: their realistic approaches to race, wealth, pollution, and Armageddon. But there had always been that nagging question: How do they reproduce?

With this questions answered, Republicanism became sexy. For the first time, the right made the centerfold.

Poppy was inspired during these "labors of love" by Yellow Rose. She had bought a small townhouse on 16th Street, near the Soviet Embassy. They spent many happy hours experimenting with and refining the Sex Manual. In fact, it was originally her idea.

One useful addition she brought to the process was a compact video camera—at that time a very unusual piece of equipment. They had many a merry chuckle reviewing their "performances." Over the months she amassed a large collection of amusing and intimate tapes.

Though the exciting, vital, and statuesque Yellow Rose was the antithesis of a homebody, she did do some of the little chores a busy man needs doing. She tidied up his briefcase every night, went through his suit pockets before taking them to the dry-cleaners, and made discreet visits to his office in the EOB. She became—as she joked—his "Concepcion," keeping his desk, closets, files, and wall safe neat. She changed his flowers and light bulbs every time she visited, and rewired his sound system.

In August 1974, Gerald Ford became President. With his jolly wit, sagacious tenacity, and home-spun intelligence, he soon became Poppy's new idol. And he looked fair set to become Poppy's new mentor, too. But it was not to be.

One day, after thinking for several weeks, President Ford decided to hold a straw poll to pick his new Vice-President. He polled prominent Republicans throughout the land. The result was 255 votes for Poppy, and 181 for Nelson Rockefeller, the pinko billionaire who had sold out his conscience and excellent background to curry favor with low-life liberals.

Unfortunately President Ford was mildly innumerate. He believed that any number with "8" in it was bigger than a number with only "5" in it. Before the mistake could be caught, the wealthy com-symp had been declared Vice-President.

But the sneaky snakes in the grass had not finished their spineless work.

Poppy simply loved the new British comedy series *Monty Python's*

> **Unfortunately President Ford was mildly innumerate. He believed that any number with "8" in it was bigger than a number with only "5" in it.**

Poppy's uncanny resemblance to British actor John Cleese led to a brief affair with Margaret Thatcher.

Flying Circus. He'd always been a great Anglophile—quite natural for someone who was 343rd in line for the British throne.

In particular he admired John Cleese, to whom he bore an uncanny resemblance. He developed a habit of bursting into long diatribes in a bad English accent. He claimed he was a mouse and had been a cheese addict. He bought a stuffed parrot, which he banged on his staffers' desks, yelling that it was "a dead parrot, a deceased parrot, an EX-parrot!"

One day in late December, Poppy startled his staff and influential party members by circulating a highly controversial memo. It announced that Republicans would henceforth belong to Monty Python's Flying Republican Party. It also called upon President Ford to establish a Ministry of Funny Walks.

It was an extraordinarily courageous and innovative proposal. But Poppy's faceless, spineless foes sensed their moment had come. They struck.

Several hours later Poppy was summoned to the Oval Office. The President, reading slowly and carefully from something under his desk, thanked him for his tireless efforts on behalf of the President and the Party. He had earned a long vacation, which he should enjoy before resuming his stellar political career. The President suggested a quiet, controlled environment where there was no traffic with its disturbing smog and noise, no distracting politicians trying to shout one another down, no disorienting protesters with their crude insulting signs.

The choices were: the psychiatric wing of St. Elizabeth's or Beijing. ■

★

The Republican Sex Manual

The Chairman's A to Z

Republican Foreplay

Abortion: *What is abortion?*
Excuse me?

Coming: *I recently had sex with a Democrat by mistake. When we were through she asked me, "did you come?" The answer to this seemed obvious, since I was present in the room. What did she mean?*
A: "Come" is Democrat for "orgasm" Republicans say "go," as in "did you go?" or "I just went" or (very rare) "Boy did I go good!"

Conception: *What is conception?*

A: For most Republicans "conception" is the Christian name of a Honduran maid with no green card. It can also refer to making babies. There are two theories of conception, **the evolutionary** and **the creationist.** The evolutionists (often scientists and secular humanists) say that when a man "goes" in his wife, his whatsis combines with her whosis to make a small amoeba-like thing, which then evolves through all the stages of life until it becomes a baby.

Creationists holds that God makes a baby puts it in a woman's tummy (or anywhere else He pleases, like a cabbage patch) and that's that.

Cunnilingus *What is cunnilingus?*
A: Cunni-Lingus is small feeder airline in the Republic of Ireland connecting Connemara with Dublin.

Fellatio *What is fellatio?*
A: Something that can only be handled by a "fella," and then only by one who is a high Administration official and/or CEO of a Fortune 500 company.

Foreplay *Democrats are always discussing foreplay. What is it?*
A: There are several forms of Republican foreplay. Its aim is a) To delay as long as possible the inevitable moment when sex has to occur. b) To cool off the partners prior to sex so that minimal mental and physical disruption occurs *(See diagram on opening page).*

The man slowly removes his jacket, tie, and pants. He folds pants making sure creases are

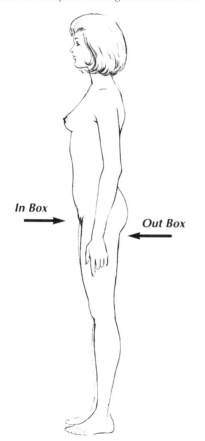

In Box

Out Box

straight. He rolls tie smaller end first and places same in left jacket pocket. He lines up shoes (side by side) with nearest wall. He files nails carefully and removes any nose-hairs.

If the female needs further foreplay (e.g., if panting, whimpering, begging, and pleading exist), the man now removes his shirt and socks. He folds both slowly, placing folded socks in the exact center of the folded shirt and placing both on nearest chest of drawers with the right angle of the bottom corner of the shirt exactly two inches from the corner of the chest-top (Take time to get this right.)

NOTE: Keeping a small iron handy to iron each garment can extend foreplay still further.

Onanism Is Onanism anything like other -isms, e.g. capitalism?
A: Onan was a character in the Bible. He had a habit of "going" by himself rather than in the proper receptacle, Mrs Onan. Onanism is risky because bizarra results like blindness and lycanthropy can result. It is permissible in certain highly selective situations: e.g., while serving one's country on board ship, or when you strike oil.

Orgasm (Republican, male) *How do I know if I've had an orgasm?*
A: If you feel exactly as if you:
a) Just made a hole in one.
b) Just inherited 1000 shares of General Electric Preferred.
c) Just shot and killed an intruder.

Orgasm (Republican, female) *How do I know if I've had an orgasm?*
A: Don't worry. You haven't.

Positions *What is the "missionary" position?*
A: An extremely rare sexual configuration in which the female kneels as if in prayer. It is used only in connection with fellatio.

Premature Ejaculation *My wife says I P.J. all the time. Do I?*
A: Probably. P.J. is "going" before the "missile"

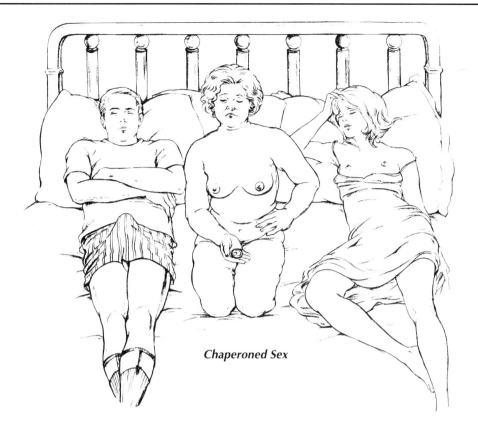

Chaperoned Sex

is in the "silo," It ocurs in 87% of all Republican sex acts. It's therefore considered normal, while "going" in situ is considered "delayed ejaculation," or D.J. P.J. is often referred to colloquially by Republlicans as "trickledown."

Prophylactic *What is a prophylactic?*
A: A rubber balloon device placed over a man's thingummy during IT. Its advantages are

a) it curtails the giddy-making drug-like sensations that sometimes accompany "going."
b) it collects the "go" instead of letting it squirt all over the inside of your wife, making sanitary disposal and general clean-up the work of minutes instead of hours.

(**Warning:** Evolutionists believe prophylactics prevent conception. If they are right this would make their use immoral and darn your soul to Heck for all eternity).

Republicans often refer to a prophylactic as "the safety net."

Sex, Lawn *Will sex in the yard ruin my lawn?*
A: "Go," or as doctors refer to it, "semen" (no connection with the Navy) is highly toxic. It will almost certainly burn a hole in your lawn, when spilled. If you are prone to "trickledown," best use a rubber sheet for sex in the yard (under your wife). But remember—crabgrass can give you crabs!

Sex, Taxes *I am the CEO of a Fortune 500 company with tremendous demands on my time. Can I hire someone to have sex for me?*
A: Yes. The cost, including travel, entertainment, sanitary disposal, etc., is deductible. Note however that there are fiscal advantages to having your own sex. Legislation is pending in the Senate which would make it possible for heads of households to claim their sex organs as dependents.

Sex,Wife *I've noticed my wife keeps her eyes closed during sex. Why is this?*
She's asleep.   ∎

Poppy "on vacation" in Madrid in the fall of 1980.

★

Chapter 8

Watching His Assets

POPPY SAT NEAR THE FRONT OF A BAR in the Plaza Mayor, waiting for the mullah. It was September 15, 1980. Not for the first time in recent months he reflected on the monumental privilege of being born an American. Here was he, a simple country boy from Greenwich, Connecticut, on the brink of becoming Vice-President of the greatest nation in the history of the world. And he owed all to one man— **CLASSIFIED** . Everything had

changed since that drizzly Thanksgiving Day in 1978 when **CLASSIFIED** had come to see him in Houston to explain how the 1980 election would work. Literally everything. It was the kind of stuff he lived for. Behind-the-scenes back-stage undercover things that meant other things than the things people thought they meant.

Sometimes when he was having lunch with people, oafs from the Chamber of Commerce or something, he'd have to excuse himself and go to the little boys' room, lock the door, and just giggle and wiggle his whole bod and air-wash his hands at the super-deliciousness of knowing secret stuff the oafs didn't know and never would!

Ironically Poppy felt more like a spy as part of the Reagan team than he did when he was DCI, head of all spies.

Immediately on returning from his R&R in Beijing, President Ford, whose cautious judiciousness had made him Poppy's new idol, asked him to head up the CIA. This was a tremendously tricky job.

No question that knowing more than two and a half million secrets gave the DCI tremendous power. But you never knew when one would slip out—like Prime Minister Harold Wilson's testicle problem (only one) or Billy Carter's actual rank in the Klan.

He'd acquitted himself pretty

well. Perhaps the uniforms idea was a bit off base (covert Ops had gone ape-sugar over that!). And there had been the whole mole thing.

After more than a dozen section heads had told him Langley was riddled with moles, he got hold of Bar's Hammacher-Schlemmer catalog and ordered twelve dozen of those spikes you stick in the lawn that emit high-pitched tones to repel the little critturs. Boy, was his face red!

Lawns looked great, though!

He was always getting dragged up to the Hill to answer dumb questions about stuff he couldn't possibly keep track of like who Pinochet or the Shah had tortured to death that week, or which Swiss numbered account went with who (Marcos mostly).

There were sweet moments. Sending out female operative with a handbag full of poppers. Mission Not So Impossible: Get into Nelson Rockefeller's pants. What was her name again? Rhymed with "Reagan" Big girl. Vulgar too. But—she got the job done.

The Big Surprise: While he and Bar were in Beijing, Yellow Rose had disappeared off the face of the earth. Poppy looked her up in agency personnel files and whattayaknow? She'd been KGB all along! Nine months earlier the agency nailed her but she got a tip-off and slipped through their fingers into Mexico. Phew! That little chippie! He tried to count up how many secrets he'd told her—must've been thousands. What the hey—he had zillions of others.

But he'd miss her. The way she teased him about not having a rear-end. That thing she said that got him so hot—"Ream my lips!" He spent a

few hours under the stars at Kennebunkport thinking about that.

What really bothered him was that evil creepo Andropov sitting in the Kremlin watching a videotape of her and Poppy do the-Elephant-and-the-Monkey thing from the Kama Sutra.

Better not tell Reagan about that!

But it wasn't just Poppy that had been penetrated by commies. Langley had too. One day, right after he'd used it, the toilet in his private washroom blew up. If he'd been one of those lingerers he'd've been cat's-meat. One lunchtime he threw his pooch, C. Fred Mertz, a piece of chicken he'd just had sent up from the cafeteria and the dog dropped dead. Things routinely fell off his car as he was driving home—steering wheel, brakes, engine, and so on. He switched to an agency limo but the driver blew up.

That was the last straw. He told President Carter he wouldn't stay on for love or money. Not that the weenie wanted him to, anyway. *His* first choice for DCI was Jane Fonda.

The single most exciting thing about being DCI had been drugs. (Fighting them that is.) The President of Panama, Omar Torrijos, was a terrific asset. He once told Poppy that drugs were a time-bomb and Panama was the neck of the hour-glass through which they were flowing. Or something like that; his English wasn't so hot and he seemed to have a permanent cold—always sneezing in the middle of sentences.

He sent his chief of security up to DC in 76 to have lunch with the DCI and fill him in on the Central American drug scene, and wouldn't you know? it turned out to be Señor

The Director of Central Intelligence meeting with Panama's Head of Security in 1976. The photo was recovered during Operation Just Cause.

Midget-Hustler from Poppy's Skull and Bones days. Small world!

Lunch was fascinating! Noriega had hair-raising intelligence about drug activities in Central America. Seemed about the only place that was clean was Panama. And the most amazing people had transshipment operations in these places: the PLO, the North Koreans, the Khmer Rouge, the IRA, the Red Brigades, the Baader-Meinhof gang. All were pumping their filthy marijuana directly into America's arm. Even Gus Hall, Alger Hiss, and the Rosenberg kids were involved.

Poppy was horrified. He slapped the Midgetman on the hush-hush payroll, right then and there. And he really took a shine to Manuel. Sure the guy was puny, but, hombre, was he a live wire! The guy could do a Carmen Miranda impression without putting a pineapple on his head.

When Poppy moved back to Houston in '77, he popped down to Panama several times on business and got to know the little guy pretty well. (Had a couple of wild nights there too—Manuel had definitely moved on from midgets.)

Manuel was always saying there

★

were good people in Panama, much love and respect for the Yanquis. Much pro-American money. In fact, he said there were a lot of people in Panama who would like to see Poppy in the White House. Interesting.

Because, of course, 1980 was the time to make his move. And with the Prez gone, money might not be so easy this time around.

But then Ronald Reagan entered his life.

CLASSIFIED brought him to the Houston Thanksgiving meeting. With him was his chief associate Ed Meese, a cold fish who looked like the only exercise he'd ever taken was an enema.

He'd met Reagan before at Republican dos, but he'd been doing the goofy grandpa stuff he did on TV. Offstage he was totally different. Eyes like a gila monster, never cracked a smile, cut-and-dried. What little he and Meese said was s-word this and f-word that.

"Here's the deal" said **CLASSIFIED** **CLASSIFIED** "I want you for Veep. You do what you're told, sweep floors, and scratch backs. I'm told you also look great in blackface."

Poppy got **CLASSIFIED** drift, but who cared? Number 2! Just like that! He gave Reagan and Meese the Boyish Grin. They stared at him like he was something from Sea World.

"Most people," continued **CLASSIFIED** "think you're a fag. But we know better, don't we George? We've seen the tapes."

"Wh-what tapes?"

"Wasn't that the Elephant and the Monkey from the Kama Sutra?" asked Meese.

The Director of central Intelligence with an antique globe presented to him by Anatoly Dobrynin. The Soviet Ambassador, a close friend, asked Poppy to speak "slowly and distinctly" whenever he used the globe.

★

"But how did you...who...?"

"Casey. Anyhow the fag image is good. Give Ron something to whip you with. OK. Ron stays out of Iowa so you can knock off the deadbeats. That'll leave the two of you for New Hampshire. We set up a debate, and you take a dive. That's about it. After Detroit all you gotta do is keep your fingernails clean. Well?"

Poppy took all of one second to decide. Hardly any campaigning, everything on a plate. Plus Reagan was as old as Grant's Tomb, and you never knew ... Tears of joy sprang into his eyes.

"Yes! Yes!" he cried, shaking **CLASSIFIED** 's hand. "YES OH YES OH YES!"

Reagan looked at Meese. "Jesus H. Fucking Christ!" he muttered.

S o here he was in the Plaza Mayor, waiting for the mullah. His mission was simple. Get the hostages out right now. In return promise the Iranians anything once Reagan was in. Names of Mossad ops, nukes, anything.

In a way, it was almost too nice for Reagan, getting the boys out now. Carter might try to take credit for it. Then there was that weird thing **CLASSIFIED** had said about his people sabotaging Desert One because they didn't want the hostages out before the election. Still, what the hey!

Poppy took the mirror out of his handbag and checked his eyeliner.

"Yes! Yes!"
he cried, shaking
CLASSIFIED *'s hand.*
"YES OH YES OH YES!"
Reagan looked at
Meese. "Jesus H.
Fucking Christ!"
he muttered.

Yup, it was running. He dabbed at it with a powder-puff. Shoot, now he looked like a vampire. The café was bordered by large juniper bushes in pots. The one nearest him was Casey. It snickered.

Suddenly the mullah appeared. He was fat and wore glasses. Poppy tried to break the ice. "Excuse the dress," he grinned. "Thought it'd make you feel at home—seeing as how you wear one all the time!"

The mullah looked at him like a plate of undercooked sheeps' eyes.

Poppy got on with it: Hostages out now. Oodles of arms later.

The mullah spat. He said they'd never give Carter the CIA scum. Carter was the Great Satan, plus his initials were the same as Jesus Christ who was a stinking Jew. But if Reagan won and he gave them all the arms they wanted, the hostages would be free five minutes after he was inaugurated.

Poppy was crestfallen. He dropped his lace handkerchief.

"What do I say?" he hissed at the bush.

"Say yes, asshole."

"O.K." said Poppy to the mullah, who spat on the table and was gone.

Back at the hotel, Poppy called Reagan in California.

"I'm sorry, Ron. I promised them just the moon, but they think Carter's the Great Satan, and they absolutely will not release the boys until they know for sure he's gone." ∎

**Vice President Poppy holds an advanced econometric device used by Budget
Director David Stockman to predict fluctuations in the money supply.**

★

Chapter 9

Reagan Bull

VICE-PRESIDENT BUSH settled back in the main cabin of Air Force Two. He was on his way to Dallas to dedicate the Old Hotel Texas in Fort Worth, where John F. Kennedy had spent his last night on earth. (And where Poppy and Yellow Rose had spent many earthy nights.) The Boeing 707 had been LBJ's favorite plane. On it he'd spent the happiest two and half hours of his life, flying back from Dallas to D.C. after the tragic but necessary death of JFK.

Poppy, who was hoping to find five minutes to go "varmint" shooting, had placed his gun-case casually on a side table. Suddenly the side table slid into the cabin wall and the case clattered to the floor. From its side pocket spilled a box of what should have been long-nose .22 bullets.

But they weren't .22 long-noses! He checked each one frantically, hoping against hope. A cold hand clutched at his heart.

They were all blanks! He had given Hinckley the wrong bullets!

On Inaugural Day January 20, 1981, the forecast was for rain, but the sun broke through.

In America the forecast had been for "national malaise" but the bright moon of Ronald Reagan lit up the darkened skies.

There was much gloom to be dissipated. This was an America stultified by its young. A nation whose stomach had been turned by the "Dyspepsi" generation.

This was an America in which overweight welfare mothers with ridiculous names like Danitra lived high off the hog, while promising young exeuctives who'd spent long years studying supply-side theory were barely eking out a living on 120 Gs a year.

This was a nation grown soft and flabby. People had forgotten that America can only be No.1 when Americans look out for No. 1. That every transaction is a tiny war to be won. That the word "aggressive" is a compliment. That balls pay the bills.

This was a nation that had lost its nerve, one that was allowing anyone and everyone to butt in front of it on the crowded off-ramp of life.

This was a nation that no longer had the guts to deal with the type of individual who butts in line on a crowded off-ramp. Reach in the glove compartment and blow his stupid brains all over the passenger seat.

"**F**uckfuckfuck!" said Poppy, very quickly to get it over with.

"Jesus, Mary, and Joseph, Bush!" said National Security Adviser Richard Allen. "You sound like a fucking chicken! Try again: 'Fuck-ing Ass-hole'"

He resembled Sister Mary Joseph with a particularly thick toddler.

"F-f-f-f-" sprayed Poppy. "Ah, the heck with it!"

"The WHAT with it?" yelled Allen.

"I mean the HELL. I mean the F-WORD! Darn! Why the sugar can't I say the f-word? I'll NEVER make the team!!"

The day Poppy stood beside Ronald Reagan on the Inaugural stand, he made himself a promise. He was going to be the best darn Vice-President in history. He was going to be Ronald

Reagan the Second. That would be his contribution to the Reagan Revolution

So now the wishy-washy who'd once said that what you did in the privacy of your own bedroom was your own beeswax, providing it wasn't too disgusting, now felt gays should have rusty tailpipes hammered up their rear-ends and be thrown off a cliff.

(And he had to stop saying "gay," gosh darn it! It was "fag" or "fudge-packer"!)

To tell the truth it was kinda neat hating people and not feeling grungy about it. It was as if Ron had deregulated his feelings.

But the f-word thing eluded him.

The first Martin Luther King Day 1983. New tough-talking Reaganaut, Poppy Bush to King's widow, Coretta: "The bad news Mrs. King, is your husband's still dead. The good news is, you got the day off."

★

Daredevil Poppy was a vital cog in the brilliant plan to "assassinate" President Ronald Reagan. He even drove John "The Mad Loner" Hinckley, to his date with destiny.

Try as he would he couldn't get his lips to say F-U-C-K nice and slow, so he meant it, so everyone would know he took no prisoners.

He knew that was why they gave him these dinky little jobs to do, like getting more handcuffs for the South Florida Task Force. He knew that was why Ron still introduced him to foreigners by saying: "I'd like you to meet Vice-President Bush, who is, in every sense, Number 2."

That's why he'd jumped at the Hinckley thing when it came up.

They'd all been there in the Situation Room: Casey, Haig the Horrible, Buchanan, Meese, Allen, Stockman, Jim Baker, and of course **CLASSIFIED** who Poppy hadn't seen since the Inaugural Ball. (The real one. The one where Meese made that odd announcement. "Guys," he'd said, "anyone here who's into that homo stuff better get it out of their system tonight. Starting tomorrow, it's gonna be real dangerous.")

"Poppy," said **CLASSIFIED** "we're doing a little stock-taking here. The Reagan Revolution is a reality. People are standing taller and talking louder than ever before. Warfare is in, welfare is out. Sex has disappeared. Now. We want to enact a huge tax cut and boost defense spending to a trillion a year. To do that we have to do

★

something dramatic."

"Question," said Casey. "How did LBJ get all this commie shit passed into law?"

"Well," said Poppy, "JFK got assassinated."

"Right!" said Casey. "And that's how Ron's gonna get it passed back out again."

"By getting assassinated?" Poppy asked. His heart-rate suddenly went to 200.

"By getting *almost* assassinated." said Casey.

"Here's the script," cried Buchanan. "Ron strides to his limo. A Mad Loner skulks to the front of the crowd. Shots ring out. The leader falls. He's rushed the hospital where, smiling through his pain, he retains his legendary sense of humor. 'Honey,' he says to his grieving wife, "I forgot to duck." "Hope the doctor's a Republican," he quips to the press. Amazed surgeons discover that the bullet has lodged just ONE INCH from his great big American heart! By the skin of his teeth and the luck of the Irish, Ron pulls through! Boom! Tax-cut, Star Wars, end of welfare state!"

A Mad Loner had already been located (thanks to the FBI's National Nut Network). Poppy's role was crucial but simple. He would "conspire" with the ML to kill Ron, and provide him with the weapon and the "ammo." As the one person in the world with the most to gain from Ron's death,

> *Of course he'd be President now. For about four seconds, until Hinckley spilled the beans. Then trial, disgrace, execution. Why had he supported the death penalty, goshdarn it!*

Poppy would be ultra-convincing.

Everything had gone like clockwork. He met the Hinckley kid in the hotel. Even liked him a little. (Poppy, too, had thrilled to the virginal allure of Jodie Foster's legs in *Taxi Driver.*)

And now he'd blown it! Even as he stared in horror at the cleverly disguised gold-foil tips of the blanks, Hinckley was working his way to the front of the press section and raising that other .22 to kill the President!

When the news finally came over the radio moments later, it was even worse than Poppy had expected. Three men down. Ron rushed to the hospital.

Of course he'd be President now. For about four seconds, until Hinckley spilled the beans. Then trial, disgrace, execution. Why had he supported the death penalty, goshdarn it!

They were all there in the hospital room. Faces grim, pale. Ron lay on the bed. His eyes were closed, his face white, his hands folded across his chest. The same as ever, but somehow more peaceful. Poppy looked questioningly at **CLASSIFIED**. Slowly **CLASSIFIED** shook his head. Too late, said the grim mournful eyes.

"It was all an accident, guys!" sobbed Poppy, breaking down. "You gotta believe me! Oh Ron, Ron, dear

★

CA distraught Vice President tries to end it all in the Potomac after hearing of the botched assassination attempt.

old Ron! Why did this have to happen?"

He collapsed by his fallen leader's side. Ron sat up. "Fooled ya! Fooled ya!" yelled the President. "Nyah nyah, nyah-nyah nyah!!"

Poppy fell off the bed. Everyone cracked up.

"Not to worry, George!" said Ron, laughing. "I'm right as rain. Everything went GREAT! See, Hinckley was our man all along. Course we double-crossed him—he'll never be free another day in his life."

"I don't understand!" gasped Poppy, getting up. "Why did you need me, then? Why did you DO this to me!"

"You were the fall guy, case anything went wrong," said Casey. "Never can tell. All these Secret Service hot-dogs around."

Poppy was so mad he turned purple.

"Got one thing to say to you, Casey," he spluttered.

"What's that, Poppy old thing?"

"F-f-f-f-..."

"F-f-f-f-..., Poppy?"

"F-f-f-FUCK YOU!!"

It was the biggest round of applause he'd ever got.

Then he threw up in **CLASSIFIED**'s lap. ∎

Poppy not in Honduras in the spring of 1985, not with a contra, and not carrying arms traded for hostages.

★

Chapter 10

A Day in the Morning of America

JOURNAL OF THE VICE-PRESIDENT OF THE UNITED STATES:

April 15, 1985 7:00 a.m.: Arrive at the White House for breakfast. Meet White House C of Staff Don Regan. Proceed Oval Office with DR. Count out 27 (3 x 3 x 3) Bite-Size Wheatabix for President's breakfast. This number specified by First Lady's current astral whiz, a warlock named Wink who lives in a cave inCarmel. Not so bad as counting out the 343 (7 x 7 x 7) jellybeans for the jellybean jar. Still, only have to do that once a week, on Monday. (Just realized spooky thing: this is the number of members of the British Royal family who have to die for me to become Queen of England!)

7:10 a.m. Maid brings in juice, milk, scrambled eggs for Ron's breakfast. Taste each item make sure not laced with cyanide by Libyan agents.

7:12 a.m. Not dead. Breakfast OK'd by DR. Proceed office.

7:30–8:45 a.m. Read mail NID etc. Tripoli intercept indicates Libyans behind Ron's polyp. DCI recommends surgical strike Garden of Allah kindergarten attended by Quaddafi's twin nieces. ("Tough message no downside"). Also Qaddafi has indicated strong desire to meet Imelda and "try on all her shoes." Count leaks in *Post* for DR (211 this morning). Tot up yesterday's covert arms sales: Iran $3.8M, Iraq $4.2M, Syria $1.3M, PLO $1.2M, N/Korea $2.2M, IRA $1.1M. Authorize wire transfer to Manuel's BCCI acct Cayman Islands for transferral to Nic resistance. Pretty good haul today–$13.8M! Proceed Cabinet meeting.

8:50 a.m. Set up Cabinet meeting. Regan: prune danish, reg. no sug. Ed M: banana (peeled) Diet Coke. Casey: Box (1 Dozen) Drake's Cakes. Ron: Pez. Deaver: mixed nuts, pitcher margaritas.

CABINET MEETING TRANSCRIPT:

Present: Regan, Casey, Deaver, Ed M., Pat B., Ron, self. Special Guest J. Falwell.

RON: OK, let's get this sucker on the road.

DEAVER: Bush, you dumb fuck, I said margaritas not margarita mix... fucking tequila (UNINTELLIGIBLE).

RON: We have a special guest today. Reverend Jerry Falwell. Jerry, why not say grace?

FALWELL: Almighty Lord, shower your blessing on the ministers of your wrath gathered here, and in your mercy crush the testi-cles of their enemies.

ALL: Amen!

RON: Very inspiring!

FALWELL: And when their testicles have been reduced to bloody pulp, O Lord, SHOVE THE FLAMING SWORD OF YOUR RIGHTEOUSNESS UP THEIR UNHOLY BUTTS!!

DEAVER: A-fucking-men!

REGAN: What about this Bitburg mess?

DEAVER: What mess? The SS were fucking anti-communists. Just on the wrong fucking side.

REGAN: Well, some of us fought on the *right* fucking side, see?

CASEY: (UNINTELLIGIBLE).

DEAVER: Hey, Liverlips! Quit spraying in my drink!

PAT B.: I have a poem I've written about all this, Mr. President

One of Poppy's duties as Vice President was tasting the President's breakfast to check it hadn't been poisoned by Quaddafi's agents.

CIA chief William Casey whispering completetly inaudibly to President Reagan about Iran-contra, while Poppy tries desperately to hear whether they are subverting the constitution by trading arms for hostages, in which case he'd tell them to stop it right now.

which I think puts Bitburg in perspective

RON: Fire away, Pat!

ED M.: Yeah, fire away, Pat!

RON: Shutup, Ned!

ED M.: That's Ed, chief.

PAT B.: "Everything You Need to Know about World War II," by Pat Buchanan:

O Nazis, dear Nazis,
How come—
When you kill
Twenty mill
Of the Communist scum
And some Jews.—
That you lose?
I don't comprehend.
The End.

APPLAUSE IN ROOM

RON: Pat–as usual–you got me misty-eyed.

ED M.: Me too!

RON: Hey you, Ted or Fred or whatever. You know the meaning of the term justifiable homicide?

ED M.: No. Pre-law only went up to vehicular injury.

PAT B.: We can't let a buncha whining sheenies make national policy.

DR: Some of the biggest contributors to the Party are sheenies.

DEAVER: Isn't it 'bout time the house bought a round?

J. FAL.: Lord—I'm worried about the Deaver!

SELF: Coming up Mike!

PAT B.: I saw that button you

wore to the convention, Regan: "I LIKE KIKE"

RON: Now, now, fellas, nobody here likes Jews. But that's not the point. The point is, do we like Nazis?

UPROAR IN ROOM

SELF: Here you go, Mike.

DEAVER: Know something Bush? You kinda cute. Cuter'n mosta babes we got round here. Ever meet that egghead gash from the UN—Kirkpatrick? Jesus, what a mug on that one, huh? Closest thing we got to Lincoln.

END TRANSCRIPT)

11:45 a.m. Prepare for lunch w/First Lady, (or as she prefers, She Who Is First). Kinda chuffed about this. Come '88, gonna need her for that all-important endorsimento. But weirdo invitation: first a torn hand-written page:

...most trying time with Mr George Bush. Handsome, dashing, full of derring-do, he nonetheless seems either a heartless butterfly or unutterably dense. I would have thought the fire of my love for him would have scorched his well-chis-elled face, but he seems impervious to my longings. I have given him innu-merable openings, shooting him fiery darts of passion during receptions, but the armor of his disdain has repelled them every one! Well, I shall show him! He shall not trifle with my affections, I do declare!!

Clipped to this a typewritten note:

Dear George, this fragment was brought to my attention by a third party. I should like to discuss the con-
tents with you over lunch. Yrs., etc., She Who Is First.

Well what the heck. (I mean hell. I mean fuck.)

12:30 p.m. Arrive F/Lady priv quarters. Knock door, no answer. Rustling banging, etc. from inside. Then she opens up. Charming as all get out. Ciggy smell inside—didn't know she smoked. Wearing low-cut Adolfo with high hem. But—who wants to see?

Fancy lunch laid out. Large mar-tini (two olives!—perfecto!). Starts right in quizzing about "Letter." Had I ever seen it before? No. Did I know who from? No. Could I guess? No. Did it make me feel anything? Like what? Well, tough, manly, loved, amorous? No. Well did I like the writing at least? Couldn't say.

Suddenly she starts batting at the air. It's a wasp. I can't see it or hear it, but she's running about like whoop-didoo. She's yelling she's super aller-gic—if she's stung she'll put on fif-teen pounds in ten minutes. Try to help but NG. Can't see it.

Then she screams. It's gone down her front.

"Quick! Help me off with this dress!"

Get the dress off. She's going nuts! It's down her slip. She rips off slip. Bra and panties. Jeepers creep-ers! I'm alone with a naked First Lady!

"Poppy, it's gone. How can I ever thank you? You saved my life."

"Nothing, really. Can I get you a robe?"

"I wish I could express my grati-tude in some way."

"Please, no. Let me help you

back into your dress ..."

"C'mere, you big lug."

Is she kidding? Yikes! For one thing, the monkey-gland things didn't take. Her bod looks like one of those '20s lampshades Mumsy has in the parlor at Walkers Point.

The bathroom door's opening. Oh no! Get up, woman, get up! Someone's coming out! Jumping Jiminy Cricket! It's Frank Sinatra!

My absolute all-time number-one favorite song stylist!

"What gives, Nance? You said it was Ron!"

"I thought it was. But it was this—this monster! He tore the dress from my trembling shoulders!"

"What! I'll tear his fucking nuts off!"

"Wait. Frank. Listen. I just love your work. I'm your biggest— "

"He ripped the slip from my heaving bosom. 'Unhand me, sir,' I cried!"

Sinatra whips out a knife the size of canoe paddle.

"Wait, Mr. Sinatra. Goombah. Ol' Blue-Eyes. Let me explain..."

"My tiny screams dissolved in the musk-laden air!"

"You fuckin' animal! Thought you was a fag!"

"I am! I am! That's right! That's my whole point!"

NG. Old Silvertonsils starts chasing me around the room. I crash into a life-size statue of Ron Jr. wearing ballet tights. Ron Jr. falls on top of me, pinning my butt to the floor. Wonderboy from

Hoboken advances.

"Lust maddened him like a beast! 'Oh save me Franco,' I cried, 'save me!'"

Actually *she* saves *me*, because she flings herself at Sinatra and sticks to him like Velcro. He can't budge— except for his knife-hand. I squirm out from under Ron Jr. and hoof it through the door a split second ahead of the knife.

I run. Behind me, the sound of She Who Is First having something I thought Republican ladies never had.

7:00 p.m. The event of the year. The Contra Party!

The White House basement looks stunning! Big sign reads: WEL-COME TO THE CONTRAPUBLI-CAN PARTY! Jungle camp theme. Everyone gets a headband and ban-

Welcome to
THE BANANA REPUBLICAN PARTY!
April 15th 1985
Meet our brave contras!

Minutes after Iran-contra is announced at a White House Press Conference, Poppy helps Colonel North remove his priceless collection of *Mad* magazines from the National Security Council Offices.

dolier with little gifties where bullets should be. Guns, jeeps, banana palms etc. ... Drinks served in canteens. Banners everywhere say: CONTRAS SI! SANDI-NO! Cute pics of elephants in headbands doing funny stuff (e.g., cutting Nora Astorga's knockers off with a machete). Behind bandstand HUGE blow-up of Ayatollah with sign: OUR FOUNDER!

Everyone's here. Casey, McFarlane, Poindexter, Secord, Gates, Clair George, Elliot Abrams, Fiers, Gregg, Motley, Cord Meyer, Menges, Clarridge, and a dozen others from the NSC and the CIA. The ragheads too: Prince Bandar, from across town, and they've flown in Hashemi, Ghorbanifar, even Kashoggi over there chatting up Fawn Hall. Good luck Adnam, she's taken.

And of course the heroes of the hour, two dozen ACTUAL contras. Wonderful earthy guys, all beards and headbands. Commander Zero, natch, and Adolfo Colero. (Funny how Adolfo keeps coming up today).

Apparently the guys have been out at Langley learning how to do a weenie roast. That is, roast the actual weenies of captured Sandinistas. OUCH!

The evening heats up. Mucho ron, and I don't mean Reagan. But finally the Great One gets up. Terrific speech: "We've done it, we're over the top" (actually the $13.8M I sent Manuel this morning gets us an even hundred million). "We don't need Congress. This war's gone PRIVATE!"

Huge cheers. "Perhaps," says Ron

quieting down in that great way of his, "we should ask ourselves a very difficult question: Does this system work? Can we afford oversight committees and leaks and the press and congressmen and their busybodies poking their noses into the sacred business of war? When the chips are down and the stakes are forever?"

The whole place is slurping straight from the palm of his hand. "And now," says Ron, "I want you to meet the young man whose can-do, heads-up, to-hell-with-the-consequences stick-to-it-iveness got this job done! Friends I give you COLONEL OLIVERA DEL NORTE!!"

> **"Tonight we celebrate the triumph of the Reagan Revolution. We came to Washington running against the government. And tonight I announce that the government has been overthrown!"**

On comes Ollie in full-dress uniform and dark glasses! The kid looks unstoppable! The contras go crazy! As for Fawn, it's Eyes Only for Ollie!

First Ollie gives the boys a peptalk:

"Por la gloria del los Stados Unidos y la victoria contra el communismo, necesitan 'can-do guys'! Viva el 'can-do-ismo'! Solo el 'can-do-ismo' puede guarantar la victoria contra los liberales, los pinko, los artistos, los intellectuales, las faggots y las Sandinistas. EL SCUM DEL MUNDO! Vosotros son 'can-do guys'! Y El Colonel Olivera del Norte is el hombre por vosotros!!"

Well, the place goes bananas. People are stamping, cheering, tearing up the plastic palms. Now Ollie brings it home:

"Contras, ladies and gentlemen, comrades in arms. Tonight we celebrate the triumph of the Reagan Revolution. We came to Washington running against the government. And tonight I announce that the government has been overthrown! We have found a better way!

"Folks, we in the military have always known this! And many of our brothers south of the border have always known this. Let us not be too proud to call ourselves the B I G G E S T BANANA REPUBLIC OF THEM ALL! VIVA AMERICA! VIVA RONALD REAGAN!!"

The band begins to play the hottest, most finger-popping, hip-snapping samba I've ever heard! Ollie starts to sing and pretty soon everyone's got the words. They went like this:

Banana, Banana,
Banana Republicana!
Hoy y Mañana,
WE'RE BANANA
REPUBLICANS NOW!
From LA to Alabama
We say "Democracy,
Yo' Mama!"
Who needs the vote?
It only rocks the boat!
Dance the Night of
the Junta away!
Dance the Night of
the Junta away!

And darn it (I mean damn it) did we ever! ∎

President-elect Bush visits the Virginia State Penitentiary to thank Willie Horton for winning him the '88 election.

Chapter 11

Where There's a Willie, There's a Way!

FINALLY!!! HE WAS RUNNING THINGS!!! YAAAAY!!! HE COULDN'T BELIEVE IT! After all these years! HE was allowed to sit behind the desk in the Oval Office and put his feet on it and turn the lamp on with his big toe! HE got all the mikes and cameras pointed at him! All the fat pimply guys with beards and and big poles and thingummies on their heads had to run after HIM!! No more standing around two paces behind some old ninny, doing the Boyish Grin, being Young and Promising, Number Two on his way up!

He was UP! He was There! No more being Young! No more being Promising! He was Number One! He was a GROWN-UP!!

As far as the mental eye could see, there were people who had to do what HE SAID! Even if they used to boss him around! Even if they'd been ahead of him at school! Agriculture, the IRS, the Navy, the National Parks System, the Federal Deposit Insurance Corporation, you name it. He said Jump! and those tootsies had to be off terra firma!

I said Jump! buster. Read my lips!

No more Nixon! No more Ford!

No more Reagan! No more being pushed around by dandruffy geeks like Haldeman and Ziegler and that doughnut Meese.

What a slimy old fraud Reagan had been! Vulgarity on the hoof! Dreams-and-weapons-are-all-we-need, indeed! California's-the-future-of-America, indeed! Sez who? Hit the road, Jack!

He'd known all along the Reagan Revolution was a pile of owl-poop. Where was the surprise in that? When you got right down to it, the fella was a jumped-up hayseed. Who or what that was worthwhile had ever come out of Dixon, Illinois? Any decent schools there?

And now look what a mess they

★

were in! Poppy's heart bled for the poor, the homeless, the two-car-garage-less, the plenty-of-closet-space-less, the thirty-six-foot-ocean-going-yacht-less.

Some vicious bitter people were even trying to blame HIM for all this. Him, who'd fought it every step of the way. Those lousy liberals threatening to bring up that stuff about Neil and Silverado. These were the same creepos, mind you, who were always yelling and screaming about discrimination against the disabled!

Well, Neil was disabled. He was dyslexic, remember? The kid couldn't read zeroes. Thought he was lending a friend a coupla bucks, signed the note, and someone else noticed there were eight zeroes after the 2.

Was that his fault? No! Boom! End of story!

And what about the other messes Reagan left around the place? Boy, had he been HAD on that whole arms-for-the-contras thing—whoever the contras were.

The worst thing about being around Reagan was how old he made you feel. You moved slower, you thought slower, your memory went kablooey. People told him he'd met with this little slug Noriega down in Panama a few times, but darned if he could even put a face to the fella.

Jim Baker had brought it up. Produced these chits from Noriega, outlining various outlays: how much

he'd contributed to the '84 campaign, via Poppy, how much he'd skimmed "off the top" for the "contras" (see above) via Poppy, etc. etc. Sounded like a bad movie, but Jim had the originals.

So now he'd have to give Jim State.

He could do anything he liked now. HE WAS RUNNING THINGS!

Gosh, he'd hated the campaign! First he had to have that very painful testicle thing done to deepen his voice.

Then all that palaver about Willie Horton? Why? He was not a racist. He had to protect his right wing. Which he never would've worried about if Jebbie hadn't married a wetback.

Ditto the Quayle nonsense. Sure, Quayle was a poor little rich lamebrain, a Party hack, and a blithering idiot. But that made Poppy, who was often accused of exactly the same things, look great! Quayle was his Agnew.

And he'd been v. smart about the no-new-taxes thing. He got the idea from Bar doing all that work with deaf kids. See, only his voice was saying the famous words. But if you actually read his lips they were saying: "When you guys realize what deep doo-doo Reagan left the economy in, we're going to have to raise taxes."

Ask any deaf person.

That way NO ONE COULD

> ***Sure, Quayle was a poor little rich lamebrain, a Party hack, and a blithering idiot. But that made Poppy, who was often accused of exactly the same things, look great!***

At a bi-partisan military photo opportunity during the 1988 election Poppy gives up his turn in the tank to Governor Michael Dukakis.

January 1989: The Bushes move into the White House only to discover that "Nancy took everything!"

★

ACCUSE HIM OF LYING!! It was BRILLIANT!!

But now the campaign was behind him! OVER! Reagan was behind him! OVER! Few more days and the old corpse'd be outa the White House for good!

Poppy switched on the desk lamp with his big toe. It shone brightly against the gray January gloom that filled the Oval Office, casting a pool of light across his blotter. The Number One blotter in the land.

Suddenly Poppy felt very Presidential. He wiggled his toes back into the loafer and put his feet on the floor where they belonged. He got up slowly, hands clasped behind his back, and gazed out the window. He was going to be a crackerjack President! Welcome to the Bush Legend!

He flipped on the voice-corder:

Preliminary Notes for Inaugural

Message 1989:

The decks are cleared. We are ready for action! The time has come to put aside the past and go forward into the future!

(MEMO TO SELF: Amazing how the words just FLOW once you're Prez. Phew!)

The Bush Administration will sink or swim... no, no... No more of that common-man stuff. Hem! The Bush Administration will be constructed on three great pillars of policy:

GUNS! FLAGS! And VOLUNTEERS!

(Brilliant! Buh-RILLIANT! Kinda military for the guys, nicer than Reagan for the gals!)

1. GUNS. It is my belief that guns in the home are a sacred right of all Americans. Guns are also crucial to education. Only by protecting the right of every Mom and Dad to keep a .45 in the bedside drawer can

During the 1989 flag-burning controversy, Poppy selects the Old Glory that will later become a matching pair of His 'n' Hers boxer shorts.

★

An ultra-cost-conscious President, Poppy has insisted that White House aides cut their traditional three martinis at lunch down to one.

American boys and girls learn how to defend themselves against the Willie Hortons of the world. That is why I can also say that I will be the education President!

2. THE FLAG. Nothing is more precious to us Americans than our beloved Stars and Stripes. The flag is a holy symbol bathed in the blood of our fallen warriors. The red stands for the red corpuscles of their blood, the white stands for the white corpuscles, and the blue stands for the... er... well for blue blood, I guess. I intend to crusade till my dying breath against the desecrators of Old Glory, the flag-burners, the atheistic liberals, the coddlers of Willie Horton and his ilk!

3. VOLUNTEERS. I see America lit up by thousands of those little blue lights volunteers have on their cars so they can drive 135 mph down narrow country roads when they're on an errand of mercy. Very few things bring out the good side of

our great nation like a burning house or a really grisly car accident. Accidents which are often caused by unlicensed uninsured convicted black rapists in furlough programs who have nothing to lose. People like Willie Horton.

(MEMO TO SELF: try Reagan Personal Touch Story here.)

And let me remind those who pooh-pooh volunteerism that to be a volunteer takes exceptional people, exceptional courage. Just the other day I attended the funeral of a volunteer who died when the first-aid vehicle he was driving crashed into a volunteer ambulance speeding to the help of a volunteer injured in the explosion of a fire-engine operated by volunteers. That's America at its best!

Aside from these three Great Principles, what can you expect from the Presidency of George Bush? The answer to that is simple. Nothing!

I intend to be the first President in a very long time to LEAVE YOU ALONE!

A long time ago my Daddy told me I was Born to Run Things. Last November you proved him right. But he also said that Running Things doesn't mean Doing Things. It means making sure Things Run. From where I sit, Things seem to be Running just fine. Most of the people I know in Washington (where I live) and Texas (where I live), and Maine (where I live) aren't complaining. They have a roof over their heads, a couple of cars to drive, and plenty of inexpensive help.

My philosophy of government is this: If you ain't broke, don't fix it.

OK, America–LET'S GO BONE-FISHING!! ∎

★

Saddam Hussein's Mom, Madame Saddam, whose titles include "Big Imama", and "The Mother of all Mothers". For years Madame was under the mistaken impression that Poppy was pro-Iraq. Boy was her face red!

Chapter 12

Heavens, Kuwait!

AUTHOR'S NOTE: The President of the United States himself has requested that he take over the controls of this book for "The Final Descent."

WELL, LADIES AND GERMS (little joke), you all know the rest of this pretty darn inspiring story. Looking back over the first four years of my Presidency, I have much to be chuffed about. I've met my goals. Every American has a gun. Most of them have a flag. And thanks to cutting waste and fat out of industry, the volunteer business is through the roof! On the legal front, I've appointed two ardent non-activists to the Supreme Court. No one better than David Souter and Clarence Thomas, who between them barely know how to chase an ambulance.

Plus—a big plus—Clarence is a Negro. As I said to him at his swearing-in—to play the piano you need the black keys as well as the white. (Of course the black keys are much smaller and there aren't so many of them.)

We can look to Justice Thomas to wipe out the scourge of abortion. His first words after that self-same swearing-in were prophetic: "Fetus," said Clarence, "don't fail me now!"

But you don't want hear this dry-as-dust legal guff. You want to hear about my incredible war record. And

who can blame you?

In the last eight years I've won four wars: Grenada, Panama, Gulf, and Cold.

What other Republican President can say that?

Let's get out the Ouija board. Let's ask Kennedy, FDR, Johnson, Truman. FOUR WARS IN EIGHT YEARS! To put this in perspective, that's half a war a year! That's a quarter of a war EVERY SIX MONTHS!!

This is the kind of killer war schedule people expected from fellas like Ghengis Khan or Napoleon. And did Ghengis Khan and Napoleon jog two miles, go surf-fishing, play tennis, horseshoes, golf, and

★

baseball EVERY SINGLE DAY? Betcha pointy boots they didn't!

What's my secret? Simple. Always pick a country that has either no money or no bullets.

Let me explain what I mean. Take the Big One. Gulf. Right after Panama, Jim Baker wrote me a historic memo:

TO: GHWB
FROM: S/S BAKER
RE: GUARANTEEING RE-ELECTION IN '92

Here you go. Shortlist of countries EVERYONE HATES with money/bullet ratios.

IRAN: Some money, no bullets. (Just lost 8-year war.) Upside: Easy to invade. Run by priests. Downside: Get Gorby nervous. Old news. Scale of ten: 8.

CUBA: No money ('cept rubles, ha-ha!), some bullets. Upside: Near, small. Huge contribs in '92 from Miami. Downside: Bad vibes (Bay o' Pigs). Lots of hills. Old news. Scale of ten: 7.

LIBYA: Plenty money, plenty bullets. Upside: No hills. Leader lives in tent. Downside: Get Egypt nervous. Old news. Scale/ten: 6.

NEW ZEALAND: Plenty money, no bullets. Upside: Small. No army. Downside: Long trip. Lotta white people. Who cares? factor. Scale of ten: 4.

GREECE: No money, no bullets. Upside: Easy to bomb. Run by fags. Downside: White people

(technically). Pinko PM out—just lost election for having sex with woman. Scale of ten: 3.

FRANCE: Plenty money, some bullets. Upside: Whole world will love us. Downside: Most of it owned by Krauts or Brits. Scale of ten: 2.

IRAQ: Some money, no bullets (Cf. Iran, same war). Upside: Small (same pop. NY State). No hills. No Army (just lost half a million men). Downside: Good client. Good oil. Saddam does what he's told. Scale of ten: 1. (Unless you really want to be a prick. Then he goes to 9 or 10.)

Well the choice was obvious. But how could we get Iraq to do a no-no?

Jim and I had a skull session. Suddenly it hit us. We both went: HEAVENS, KUWAIT!

See, Kuwait was undercutting OPEC. Saddam was losing a bundle. He'd felt us out about teaching his brother camel-jockeys a little lesson.

Let me emphasize that I never said "yes." I'd never do that to a loyal and wealthy ally like Kuwait, hated though they are by ragheads everywhere.

Whether or not we withheld our definitive approval I can't remember. But pretty soon, the vile mustachioed dictator and his jackbooted storm-troopers were sweeping across tiny helpless Kuwait, stealing art and raping camels. Just like Hitler swept across wherever it was.

The rest is history. And, of course, so am I.

To those who say my cause was

Poppy demonstrates to reporters why Clarence Thomas is the only man big enough to fill Justice Thurgood Marshall's Supreme Court seat.

not Kuwait but reelection, I say bunk! I had a noble cause. One any loving father will cotton to: my boy Neli. ("Neli" is what we call Neil, because that's the way he writes his name.)

Neli was in trouble. The whole S&L thing. All his fault. Therefore my fault. You know how these people think.

Well, Saddam's timing was perfect. Neli has one person to thank for the fact that he's not in jail today, and his address is: PO BOX 1, Baghdad.

And to those who say that the Gulf War wasn't much more than military maneuvers using human targets, I say DOUBLE BUNK! The Gulf War was the greatest victory since Hitler and Tojo. It was the war

of the century, flawlessly executed, 100% effective, harmless to humans, and germ-free. Thanks to the Gulf War, we stand on the brink of a Brave New Order.

Now I really hate to blow my own trumpet. But here's the thing I want to underline:

I DID IT! ME!! ALL BY MY LONESOME! THE GUY THEY CALLED A WIMP, A WUSS, A MOMMA'S BOY, A LAPDOG, A HACK, AND THE NATIONAL TWIT!!! THE GUY THEY SAID SAT DOWN TO PEE!!

GEORGE JOLLY OLD HERBERT GOSHDARN WALKER BOOLA-BOOLA BUSH!!!

That's B-U-S-H. Lever on the right.

Thank you.   ∎

Epilog

Hi! Me again, the Bush boy.

Just like to say something. Just reread that last chapter. Could see how might be seen as a teensy tad over the top. Like Mumsy always says, never talk about yourself. Let others do it. Swhy never use "I" in a sentence. If can help it.

Course lots of other fellas share credit for our mighty victory in the Gulf. Norman Schwarzenegger, for example.

But there's something else. Some of my friends like Sig Rogich and Roger Ailes, and of course Lee Atwater and the Prez when we reach them on the Ouija board—what we call the "Behind the Bush Club"—are telling me simply awful stuff.

Apparently people think times are tough out there in America. That there's a depression on.

Phew! Ouch! Color me CONCERNED!

Look—unlike many pampered young Americans, I remember the real Depression. Times were tough, tough, tough! I was five before I had my own set of golf clubs. My brother and I had to share the same sailboat for simply YEARS! But of course you know all that.

So don't tell me what it was like growing up in the Depression! I know! I was there!

The idea I want to float here is this. Are things really that bad? Or is our real problem a bunch of whiney yuppies whose parents gave them everything and who never had to want for a thing in their lives?

People like my so-called son Neil. Who frankly ought to be in jail. And who I will personally escort to the slammer and throw away the keys if that's what America wants.

Just gimme the word.

One more thought. Perhaps when people say "depression" they don't really mean money. They mean they're depressed. As in down-in-the-mouth. And who can blame them? Look at Congress, look at the environment. Look at the price of golf-balls.

But I have a message for America about the "depression." It's a lesson I learned on the job, by myself. Not a lesson I had drummed into me by a cruel but loving father during the actual Depression. It's this. However bad things get, however bleak the world looks, however hopeless the future seems, you must remember one thing:

There's always Halcion. ∎

Epilog to the Epilog

Let's get something straight.

I am not soft on drugs!

I've got one message for drug dealers. You're a DEAD BUNNY, pal! Ditto drug users! CARCAS-SES IN THE MIDDAY SUN! I'll do to you what I did the mother of all armies, OK?

Sure, that sounds tough. But who ever said GHWB couldn't sound tough? Sure, most drug dealers and users are Negroes. So what, OK? Kill 'em all and let God sort 'em out, OK?

Howdya like them apples, Mr. Pat Buchanan?

Who says this Administration can't take the low-ball hard-road approach, if that's what it takes to take charge?

Just remember America, there's always CUBA!!

OK?

And if that fails, there's plenty of Hinckleys out there!

OK?

Let's go forward to the past and kick some ass! No bog-paddy's gonna outflank me, OK?!

Over and out.

OK? ∎

Epilog to the Epilog to the Epilog

Look.

Here I am. 1992. Shoulda been a breeze. Instead ... I'm in deep fudge.

OK—skull time. Democracy means representing people, no? What they think. So the fella who's the best at democracy is the one who thinks as many of the things that people think as possible. The guy with a completely open, airy, uncluttered, this-space-available mind.

You're looking at him.

Here's the deal. Forget what I think. What do YOU think? You've got GREAT ideas. Wouldn't you like me to think what you think? I'll do it! I'll think ANYTHING you like! You just tell me what it is, and geewhiz I'll think it LIKE CRAZY!!. Hey, I'll even pay for dinner!

Wait.

COME BACK! What did I do wrong NOW? I said I'd pay for dinner!

I WON'T think what YOU think, OK? I'll get some ideas of my own and and ...

PLEASE COME BACK!

PLEEEEAAAASE!!

Shoot. ∎